CONCILIUM

Religion in the Eighties

CONCILIUM

Concilium 147 (7/1981): Church Order

THE REVISED CODE
OF CANON LAW:
A MISSED OPPORTUNITY?

Edited by

Peter Huizing
and
Knut Walf

English Language Editor
Marcus Lefébure

T. & T. CLARK LTD.   THE SEABURY PRESS
Edinburgh   New York

September 1981
T. & T. Clark Ltd., 36 George Street, Edinburgh EH2 2LQ
ISBN: 0 567 30027 7

The Seabury Press, 815 Second Avenue, New York, N.Y. 10017
ISBN: 0 8164 2347 4

Library of Congress Catalog Card No.: 80 54389

Printed in Scotland by William Blackwood & Sons Ltd., Edinburgh

Concilium: Monthly except July and August
Subscriptions 1981: All countries (except U.S.A. and Canada) £27·00 postage and handling included; U.S.A. and Canada $64.00 postage and handling included. (Second class postage licence 541-530 at New York, N.Y.) Subscription distribution in U.S. by Expediters of the Printed Word Ltd., 527 Madison Avenue, Suite 1217, New York, N.Y. 10022.

CONTENTS

Part III
Missed Opportunities?

Communication

Editorial

AT THE time of the writing of this editorial—the beginning of May—it is not yet certain when the *Lex Ecclesiae Fundamentalis* (LEF) and the new Code of Canon Law will be promulgated. The latest edition of *Informations Catholiques Internationales* mentions Giancarlo Zizola, a well-known Italian 'vaticanista' as saying that it will take place at Pentecost—the 'old' Code was promulgated at Pentecost 1917! In Rome, at the end of March, Christmas was thought of as a more likely date on which all preparations for the promulgation would possibly be completed. In either case one thing is certain: this issue of *Concilium* will not have any influence on the contents of the new legislation, even if the latter should obtain force of law only one year after promulgation, like the Code of 1917.

Why, then, this issue?

Hervé-Marie Legrand concludes his excellent study entitled 'The Church as an Institution. Theological and Juridical analyses' (in *L'Eglise: institution et foi*, Brussels 1979) as follows:

'When Paul VI recently gave his directives for the reform of canon law he declared: "The task of revising canon law cannot be reduced to a correction of the previous Code, a better ordering of its contents, by adding what seems opportune and cancelling what no longer applies." This would lead one to think that with these words the pope invited the editors to undertake a task which would necessarily involve the effort of thoroughly re-studying the concept of the previous Code. For the pope goes on to express the wish that the new Code of Canon Law may "express more clearly the spiritual character of the juridical activity which results from the Church's sacramental nature and is performed in the community of the Church. And the Church, composed of numerous members, is one in the Holy Spirit who is given to all her members at baptism and additionally to the members of the hierarchy through sacramental ordination (. . . .). Consequently the new Code of Canon Law should avoid the danger of that pernicious separation between the Spirit and the institution, between theology and law".

Well, then, if we look at the preparatory work done so far, it seems that this has been restricted to the narrower hypothesis, the one the pope wanted to exclude.

All the same . . . should this be for us a reason to criticise its promulgation? At the present stage of fundamental reflection on canon law it could be just as well, *salvo meliori judicio*, be a sign of wisdom. A blue-print for a *Lex Ecclesiae Fundamentalis* would seem to be premature in many respects; would it not be better, instead of officially recognising a new Code of law which at the moment of its publication would already be inadequate, to stick to a provisionally up-dated Code of law which does not involve the danger of obstructing a work which is to make far-reaching contributions of an ecclesiological, pastoral and ecumenical nature, and which can only be thought of as a long-term project? At any rate, as things are at this moment, rapid revision and fundamental revision seem to exclude one another.' (translated from a Dutch version of the French original as published in: *Archief van de Kerken*, 35 (1980) 334 ff.).

Consequently this issue is not meant as a criticism of the promulgation of what could be rightly considered a 'provisionally up-dated legislation', but as a contribution to the 'long-term' project that has as yet to start. With this purpose in mind we look for an answer to the question: 'What did Church leaders, popes and bishops, expect from a new Code of Canon Law before, during and after Vatican II?' (Provost). Our investigation is also helped on its way by an inventory of reactions to the drafts for a new legislation arranged according to different view-points: to which sections have canonists from different countries reacted critically? (Huysmans); what attitude does a country like Poland, a homogeneous Catholic country under a communist régime, take up vis-à-vis the revised legislation? (Sobański); what is the attitude of the Oriental Churches? (Khoury about the legislation on the election of bishops); how should they be judged from an ecumenical point of view? (Lengsfeld).

Since it was generally expected that a revision of canon law would aim at translating the spirit of Vatican II into ecclesiastical juridical terms, it is and remains an essential task of the science of canon law to compare the juridical developments, and first of all those contained in the new legislation, with the ideas of the Council. The second section of this issue contains some contributions to this task in relation to some important subdivisions of the Code: the position of the faithful (Komonchak); Book II on the people of God (Green); ecclesiology (Rikhof) and the 'religious life' (Cody).

A third section contains some contributions on special subjects affecting the new canon law: how far can traditions of the history of canon law contribute to its revision? (Zapp); what does the idea of 'catholicity' mean for the development of canon law? (Winninger); and finally, how can a juridical language form a sufficiently firm basis for the juridical ordering of a community and yet at the same time be receptive to new developments? (Potz).

By way of yet another contribution to the 'long-term' work that remains to be done we would like to pause here for a brief reflection on the *ecclesiology* of the new Church legislation.

The nucleus of the new ecclesiastical legislation consists of prescriptions concerning the structure of the Church. In order to understand the radical changes introduced by this legislation in the field of ecclesiology, we should first of all consider its pronouncements on the relation between the pope and the bishops. In many respects it shows momentous changes of accent, if we compare the decrees of the Second Vatican Council with the prescriptions of the LEF and the new Code (Rikhof). Whereas, Chapter III of the 'Dogmatic Constitution on the Church' is entitled: 'The hierarchical structure of the Church, with special reference to the episcopate', by which it emphasises the importance of the College of Bishops for the universal Church, the LEF and the new Code are out to guarantee in as far-reaching a way as possible, the 'potestas' of the pope. It strikes one as curious that the LEF and the new Code are introduced as the juridical results of the Second Vatican Council, because since the First Vatican Council no official ecclesiastical texts have been written which so heavily accentuate the primacy of the pope as do these two. On many points even the Codex of 1917 hands down the venerable old traditions of the Church on the relation between the primacy and the episcopate in a more adequate and correct way.

This holds good in particular for the legal position of an ecumenical council. Whereas the old Code deals with it after the canons on the papacy, the new Code does not contain a single prescription on the ecumenical council, and in the LEF it is presented, after the exposition on the Synod of Bishops and the cardinals, as a juridical institution totally dependent on the pope. Characteristically, in the new Code the place formerly reserved for the Council is now occupied by the Synod of Bishops, which for its composition is under the decisive influence of the pope. Also a comparison of the wording of the old Code with that of the new reveals unmistakable tendencies: the old Code says that the pope possesses supreme and complete power of jurisdiction and that an ecumenical council possesses supreme power over the universal Church (cc. 218, par. 1; 228, par. 2). The LEF now lays down that the pope possesses the 'highest, full, immediate and universal power over the Church', while it says of the College of Bishops that together with its head and never without it, it is also bearer of the highest and full power over the universal Church; but this power can be exercised only with the consent of the pope of Rome (c. 29, pars. 2 and 3). Moreover, there is the prescription of c. 34, par. 2, of the LEF, according to which this universal ecclesiastical competence only concerns the teaching office and the pastoral government; so it does not include the complete governing power.

For the rest the language used in these two juridical documents is apt to cause astonishment (Potz). What a change in the mode of expression since the times of Vatican II! For not only has the pastoral language of the Council been exchanged for the technical terms of juridical language. This is understandable and inevitable. No, these documents contradict the intentions of an assembly which we still believe was inspired by the Spirit. Whereas the Council speaks of *munus*, of service of those ordained to the people of God, these juridical documents prefer to use the concept of *potestas* (power, mandate). Whereas the Council placed the ministry of sanctifying (*munus sanctificandi*) before the ministry of teaching and governing, the new Code inverses this order: in the first place full attention is given to the ministry of governing, and this is done, believe it or not, under the title 'On the People of God'; only after that do we find the books dealing with the ministries of teaching and sanctifying. In this context LEF emphasises that 'the rightful and proper exercise of all the ministries is regulated by the ministry of governing' (c. 55, par. 2). In an almost inflationary manner the Code and the LEF use the concept of power, *potestas*, very specially so when it is a question of the juridical position of the pope. We really wonder what has happened to the language of collegiality. Who can be reached by this kind of language? We are thinking of the younger generation in our Church, but also of our colleagues in the ministry and the numerous lay persons who are engaged in the service of the Church of Jesus Christ, and we cannot help asking ourselves what on earth they can do with such a language and such a mentality which thinks and speaks in categories of 'sacred powers'. In our opinion the new Code does not speak a language which can be understood by the people of our Church. Its language and also the mentality pervading it seem strange and problematic. Moreover the linguistic and terminological changes introduced by these new juridical documents in comparison with the corresponding pronouncements of Vatican II are of such weight that we have to speak of a one-sided, even ideological accentuation of the Council decrees.

We have to conclude that both these juridical documents of the Catholic Church, the Code and the LEF, which are meant to form one integral whole, confirm practically all the objections that have been expressed for many years, also and in particular in circles of professional canonists, especially in relation to the dubious project of a fundamental law for the Church. The Code and the LEF are both based on an ecclesiology of the *societas perfecta*, which was not only alien to Vatican II, but to which the Council opposed the image of a pilgrim Church as the people of God. It occurs to us that the choice of this static representation of the Church was born out of a deep-seated fear; a fear of any form of change and development in the law and structures of the Church. We meet these static representations particularly in the prescriptions on the primacy of the pope; certain aspects of an historical development, which can after all be discerned behind these gradually evolved structures, apparently go unnoticed. Otherwise the formulation of numerous canons would have been much more reserved and differentiated. What is worse, certain contents and pronouncements of the Code are wrongly titled. When for example we find the title 'On the People of God' introducing Book II of the new Code, which describes the hierarchical structures of the Church in a completely traditional fashion, this title covers at most the introductory canon 201; for the rest practically no mention is made of the people of God, but only of those who exercise authority over this people. Consequently, it would have been more correct to give this book the title: 'On the ministry of Governing'. In this matter the writers of the LEF have been much more consistent. Whereas in the 1971 draft of the LEF chapter I still had the title 'The Church of the People of God'—and no one could quarrel with this—in the 1976 draft 'the People of God' was dropped. This, too, was perfectly consistent because all theological pronouncements on the Church as the people of God had been dropped from the text, in order to bring out more clearly and stringently those that were juridically relevant. The only thing the authors seem to have forgotten is that as a result of this operation we are now left with a dead body.

What is left after so many years of constant changing and intertwining is the organisational model of the Church of the primacy, and a statute for the ministry of the clergy. The new starts made in ecclesiology by Vatican II were pushed back step by step, or changed beyond all recognition, and this was done with an obvious singleness of purpose. The increasing importance of the laity in the ministry of the Church was practically ignored. They are only tolerated as stop-gaps and as a last resort. For this purpose c. 275 contains a kind of tiered model, indicating on what conditions lay persons can also be used in the service of the Church.

We do not deny that on specific points there have been improvements in comparison with the old Code. All the same we should ask ourselves what effect such welcome reforms will have, if the spirit of these juridical documents is marked by fear and a lack of realism. To give one example: if, on the one hand, local churches, represented by their bishops, are exhorted by Rome, time and time again, to practise 'communio', but, on the other hand, they are provided with no real organs of consultation to enable them to consult with the pope *collegially* with the prospect of being listened to, we cannot take it for granted that the local churches will resign themselves passively to this situation. We should rather expect the development, outside this juridical system, of useful structures, which in the process of their growth will naturally lead to continual and painful clashes with this Code of law. Was not an opportunity missed of translating Vatican II's vision of the collegiality of the pope and the bishops into juridical structures and into efficient ones at that? Moreover, for those who belong to this Church but do not fulfil any ministry in it, this Code of law will bear no relation to the reality in which they live. And could we not say that in addition the authors have neglected to combine in an adequate and practicable way the vision of the Council and the juridical reality of many local churches?

But can a Church order really content itself with being an organisational model for a Church of the primacy and a statue for the ministry of the clergy? Mistrust is always a bad counsellor. But mistrust of the bishops and mistrust of the laity were the counsellors of the editors of the LEF and of the new Code. The consequences of this legislation will be detected only too soon in the juridical reality of our churches.

A second ecclesiological characteristic of the Church that will need to be studied for a renewal of her Church order is her *sacramental structure*, which is necessarily, too, the structure underlying her juridical order. For this aspect, too, we refer to the above-mentioned study by Hervé-Marie Legrand.

For the renewal of the juridical order of the Church it is absolutely necessary to restore to full life, not only in theology, but also in the sense of faith of the Church members, and in the juridical order of the Church, the insight of the early Church into the fact of the Church being a 'communio' and the vision of the ancient theologians, including Thomas Aquinas, taken up once more by Vatican II, that 'the Church is built up by the sacraments' and that the Church is essentially a Eucharistic community. For the real and active presence of Jesus and his Spirit in the community of the Church is not only the object of individual piety and 'sanctification', but the foundation for the existence and the construction of the community of the Church itself. It is through this presence that the community comes into being and is maintained, in other words: this efficacious presence constitutes the 'basic law' of the Church, the *Lex Ecclesiae Fundamentalis*; only after this come the hierarchical and the remaining juridical structures of the Church. For a fuller explanation of this it is sufficient to point to a few truths of faith handed down by tradition.

It is clear that for every type of community a fundamental juridical datum is the authority on which someone becomes a member of this community, and on which, as a result, the community is constituted. Now it belongs to the sacred tradition of the Church that no one can become a member of her community on his own authority or any other human authority, neither on the authority of the whole Church nor that of the popes or the bishops. It can only be done through an act performed in the name of the Father, the Son and the Holy Spirit and in the power of Jesus' redemption. No human institution has under its control the coming into being of this community. For that reason the juridical act of baptism cannot be repeated and is inviolable. The same holds good for the consolidation of baptism, or confirmation, the effect of which is perhaps similar to becoming legally of age in the secular juridical order. The same again holds good to the highest degree of the Eucharist, in which the community of the Church accepts, confesses and lives in a real way its existence in the Lord. It holds good for the sacrament of penance, in which the communion which was broken through human sinfulness is restored.

The same holds good as well for ordination as leader or president of the community. He, too, cannot be simply appointed or chosen, but only be put in charge in the name and by the power of the Lord. Since also the authority structure of a community belongs to its constitutive elements, and since authority in the Church can only be exercised in the name of the Lord, who is her supreme authority, the appointment to such authority has been understood from the earliest days of the Church to be appointment in His name. This explains why every ordained person remains responsible for his governing and presiding, firstly and decisively, to the Lord.

Which does not mean that an ordained minister could, appealing to his capacity of 'vicar of Christ' or as 'another Christ', or as 'dispenser of Christ's grace', take up a position contrary to the community. If the hierarchical clerical order were itself to be presented as cause and foundation of the existence, continuity and and unity of the Church 'by means of the administration of the sacraments'; if therefore the sacramental structure of the Church or the presence and efficacy of Jesus and His Spirit, creating community, were to be subordinated to the sacerdotal hierarchy, then the faith in this sacramental presence and efficacy would be mutilated. The sacramental structure of the Church is and remains her essential basic structure, and it is only in the service of that structure that faith in the office of the ministry can be understood.

When in the light of all this we consider the structure of the new—and at the same time old!—Code of Canon Law, we must come to the following conclusion. The first book, about general norms, already contains the complete structure of the juridical order consisting of laws, customs, prescriptions, acts of authority, power of authority, ecclesiastical ministers, etc. In the second book, about the people of God, we find the complete sacerdotal hierarchy from pope to curate, religious associations (in the wider sense) and other ecclesiastical associations. In other words: the whole Church, with her juridical order and articulations, appears as already existing and complete. Only then follows the third book, in which the 'task of teaching'—*munus docendi*—of this Church is described, and after that the fourth book, about her 'task of sanctifying'—*munus sanctificandi*. The first part of this book deals—at last—with the sacraments, 'instituted by Christ and entrusted to the Church as being acts of Christ and the Church'; signs and means by which the faith is expressed and strengthened, cult is offered to God and the sanctification of the people is effected; they contribute therefore powerfully to the emergence, the consolidation and the manifestation of the ecclesiastical community (c. 794).

Consequently in the line of thought and in the system of this Code the sacraments are means by which a hierarchically structured Church, which pre-exists, whole and entire, fulfils her task of sanctification. Nothing is left here of the fundamental significance and efficacy of the sacraments as constitutive elements of the Church and as underlying her growth into a community and her juridical order; nothing is left either of the essentially Eucharistic communion of the ancient Church. And the consequences are grim enough. The most obvious of them is that the Church order is not built up from and around the fundamental, constitutive, sacramental acts of the community of faith, and as a result not from the local church in which this sacramental order takes place and is experienced directly, determining the position of the faithful in these churches; but that the whole Church order is based on the hierarchically structured ecclesiastical 'society', which as a result occupies the leading position in the system.

Thus the elaboration of the sacramental structure of the Church order, with all its consequences, belongs to the long-term task that awaits theologians and canonists.

PETER HUIZING
KNUT WALF

Translated by B. J. Welling

PART I

Expectations and Reactions

James Provost

The Revised Code of Canon Law: Expectations and Results

OVER twenty years have passed since Pope John XXIII called for the *aggiornamento* of the Code of Canon Law.[1] The results of thousands of hours of work will shortly become law for the Latin Church.[2] The merits and deficiencies in the new Code will appear more clearly if we refresh the expectations expressed as the work of revision was announced and eventually got underway. The expectations of popes and bishops will form the basis for this study, since their hopes raised legitimate expectations among all the people of God.

1. IDEAS ON REFORM OF THE CODE BEFORE JOHN XXIII

The idea of revising the Code of Canon Law is not new. When promulgating the Code in 1917 Pope Benedict XV set up a Commission to add or revise canons as the need might arise.[3] The process has never been used, and such was the respect for the 'juridical perfection' of the first *Codex Iuris Canonici* that only popes themselves have ordered the few deletions made to date.

There were a few voices, even from the early days of the Code era, calling for change. Their proposals focused mainly on standardising the terminology, resolving conflicts between various canons, or otherwise improving the document. It became clear that it was not popular with curial authorities to suggest touching the *Codex* even when proposals were couched in very respectful terms.[4]

Teaching canon law at all levels, even in graduate schools, shifted after the 1917 promulgation to become almost exclusively an exegesis of the Code text.[5] This tended to reinforce the atmosphere of respect for the Code and to dampen any efforts to revise it, much less to propose a major renewal of the law itself.

2. POPE JOHN XXIII AND POPE PAUL VI

Pope John's proposal to touch the Code is all the more startling against this backdrop. He called not merely for correcting inconsistencies and improving the use of language, or even for a 'revision' to incorporate decrees issued since the Code. As the

3

ultimate step in a three-fold programme for Church renewal, the new pope called for an *aggiornamento* that would crown a reform effort beginning in a diocesan synod for Rome and an ecumenical council for the Church universal.[6]

For John, *aggiornamento* does not change the core of Catholic doctrine and discipline, but makes it more adapted to the times. John spoke frequently of making the light of the gospel more visible through bringing the resources of the Church to bear on issues of the modern age, with the renewal of canon law a key element in putting this into practice.[7]

Canon law in the Johannine pontificate was seen as the practical application of faith within the Church institution. In describing what to expect from the coming Council, Cardinal Tardini, Secretary of State and responsible for initial preparations for Vatican II, focused on the connection between renewal in the Church and the Code. 'The principal goal for the Council will be especially the discipline of the Church, those provisions of the Code of Canon Law which can be changed, and then the whole range of Catholic life.'[8]

John's successor developed a more theological perspective on Church law. For Pope Paul, canon law is rooted in the gospels and must be informed by the Spirit, a law which should be an instrument of grace and a dynamic plan for action. Law participates in the sacramental nature of the Church as part of the external sign of the inner life of God's people. Paul VI saw theology and law as closely related and called for a new Code based not on civil codes and juridicism, but on a deeper theological appreciation for the ordering of Church life.[9]

Aggiornamento appeared in a new setting with Paul. It became the task of implementing the spirit and decrees of Vatican II.[10] He continued to expect the renewal of the Code would crown the work of *aggiornamento*. It 'cannot mean simply improving the earlier Code by introducing a more appropriate order of material, adding what seems worthwhile and omitting what is no longer relevant. Rather the Code must become an aid to contemporary Church life in the age after Vatican II'.[11]

In his directions to the Commission for the Revision of the Code, Paul called for a law 'adapted to the needs of the people of God and to the new spirit characteristic of the Second Vatican Council, which demands that the primacy be given to pastoral concerns'.[12] It is to be neither an uprooting of all that is past, nor some abstract structuring of Church life according to a particular system of law-making, but primarily a means 'to confirm and safeguard that new and genuine drive to renewal of Christian living which the Second Vatican Council desired and promoted'.[13]

In sum, the expectations of the two popes who called for and directed most of the work of revision are quite clear. The Code is to be renewed, not merely reorganised; it is to breathe a new spirit, the spirit of the Second Vatican Council; it is to be responsive to the pastoral needs of the times rather than an abstract legal theory or juridical systematisation.

These popes seem to be speaking from the same insight Yves Congar urges in analysing true and false Church reform in the past. Genuine reform touches the institutional dimension of the Church. Unless a reform movement moves from moralising and affects the very structures of Church life, it is not a genuine Church reform. So with the current reform effort, it will not succeed as Church reform if it does not mould the new Code.[14]

3. EXPECTATIONS OF THE BISHOPS

The popes looked to the revision of the Code to continue the renewal begun at Vatican II. To clarify the bishops' expectations it will be necessary to look first at what they expected before the Council, their developing expectations during the Council, and an important post-conciliar discussion on expectations for the new Code.

(*a*) In line with Cardinal Tardini's observation about the pastoral and disciplinary thrust of the Council, bishops submitted primarily disciplinary suggestions for the Council to discuss. The analytic synopsis of these pre-conciliar suggestions devotes 85 per cent of its pages to matters of canon law and only 15 per cent to doctrinal and moral issues.[15] Some suggestions touched on the revision of the Code as such: simplification of the laws and legal language, more pastoral orientation, decentralisation which would permit national groups to adapt the law to local conditions. Special concern was expressed about marriage legislation.[16]

Juridical issues continued to surface as the Preparatory Commissions did their work, resulting eventually in lists of items to be referred to the Commission for the Revision of the Code since not all these details could be taken up in the Council hall. So extensive were the desires expressed by individual bishops for various reforms in law and discipline that a similar process was followed during the course of the Council itself.

(*b*) Three sources illustrate the position of the Council on the revision of canon law: the Council documents themselves; the appendices to two schemata; and the general spirit or 'mind' of the Council.

Three documents explicitly require the revision of the Code to be guided by their contents: the Constitution on the Liturgy (§ 128), the Decree on the Pastoral Office of Bishops (§ 44), and the Decree on the Lay Apostolate. This last document is quite explicit: 'All [that is contained in this Decree] should be regarded as norms in the revision of canon law as it pertains to the lay apostolate' (§ 1).

Some direct changes in canon law were made by the Council. The most striking include: the authority of the College of Bishops (*Lumen gentium* § 22); the right of all bishops to participate in an ecumenical council (*Christus Dominus* § 4); establishment and authority of episcopal conferences (*CD* § 38); dispensing powers of bishops (*CD* §. 8*b*); definition of an ecclesiastical office (*Presbyterorum Ordinis* § 20); validity of Catholic-Orthodox marriages even if only the Orthodox form is used (*Orientalium Ecclesiarum* § 18) and other rules on sacramental administration (*OE* § 12-17).

The Council fathers voted some specific expectations for the content of the new Code. The organisation of ecclesiastical regions is to be worked out in the law (*CD* § 40); the law is to set up particulars on the Senate of Priests (*PO* § 7); the standing of catechumens is to be clarified (*Ad Gentes* § 14). Appropriate canonical legislation is to facilitate the insertion of the faith into institutions and customs of various cultures (*AG* § 19).

Two schemata had significant appendices related to the revision of the law. The draft document *De cura animarum* was presented with a lengthy seven-part appendix.[17] Three sections dealt with recommendations for revising the Code on the pastoral office of bishops, the pastoral office of pastors, and relationships between bishops and religious primarily relating to apostolic work. Four other sections contained proposals for pastoral directories on the pastoral office of bishops, pastoral office of pastors, special care for particular groups, and catechetical instruction. Although this schema was later divided among other documents, the appendices were to be commented on by bishops privately and their recommendations would be sent to the Commission for the Revision of the Code and other curial offices.

The 1963 schema on the Pastoral Office of Bishops had two special appendices also designed for private comment with recommendations to be forwarded to the appropriate Commission and offices.[18] The first addressed relationships between bishops and Congregations of the Roman Curia, primarily recommending a list of more extensive faculties for bishops. The second dealt with norms to govern dealings of curial offices with bishops.

B

The content of these appendices reflects both the practical concerns of bishops and the notable focus of conciliar discussion on the rôle of bishops as such. Not much is said about the responsibilities and rights of lay persons, and sections dealing with priests and religious are concerned with strengthening the bishop's hands locally. In contrast, there are various proposals to loosen the tight rein held by the Roman Curia up until then on the initiative of local bishops and the collaborative work of bishops among themselves.

The general spirit or 'mind' of the Council is more difficult to document. It was perhaps most forcefully expressed in a speech which became a rallying point for many at the Council and which has since characterised attempts to illustrate what this 'spirit' means. On 1 December 1962, towards the end of the first session, Bishop DeSmedt of Bruges, Belgium, attacked the proposed draft document *De Ecclesia* as suffering from triumphalism, clericalism, and juridicism.[19] He called for concentration instead on the people of God as central to understanding the Church, and a revaluation of 'mother' Church in place of the juridicism evident in the document, a juridicism ranging from 'hierarchalism' in picturing the Church itself to the manner in which Church membership is determined.

Other indications of the Council's spirit with a bearing on revision of the law can be found in its general teaching. Council documents show a concern for renewal; for missionary, pastoral, and ecumenical efforts; for collegiality, subsidiarity, and local adaptation of Church life; a concern for the person, human rights, freedom of conscience, and the Church's rôle in the modern world.

There was an atmosphere of freedom, hope, and a genuine sense of expectation that the Church would make a difference as a result of the Council, both in the lives of Catholics and in the world at large.[20]

There is another side to the 'spirit' of the Council. Early in the conciliar debates it became clear there were two tendencies, even two mentalities which characterised significant groupings of bishops.[21] These soon found themselves in opposition on a wide variety of points, although it was not always possible to characterise a Council father as belonging consistently to one group or the other on every issue. This division was not created by the Council; the Council merely enabled it to surface after being underground since the 'Modernist crisis' early in the century. It came as a surprise to many Catholic faithful and the world at large, and engendered an atmosphere of distrust and tension among many of the bishops when dealing with 'the other side'. It also created a setting in which the law has been seen by one or the other mentality as the way to resolve this tension.

These two mentalities are part of the 'spirit of the Council' which is still with us. Two approaches were made during Vatican II to try to bridge the differences.[22] One was to appeal to the 'pastoral' nature of the Council; the other was to achieve consensus by careful use of diplomatic theological language.

To traditional-minded bishops, 'pastoral' had the implication of being outside the range of dogma and relating only to the practical application of Church teaching, much as they had· used a 'thesis-hypothesis' approach to cope with modern Church-State relations. This approach accepts the practical necessities of the moment, but looks forward to returning to the fullness of truth when more favourable times permit. 'Pastoral' is not law, for law must remain faithful to the fullness of truth. For more open-minded bishops, 'pastoral' defined the very nature of what the Church is, the application of the gospel to life. It is the most authentic manner to speak of doctrine and the only authentic law. Discovering they could reach agreement on wording and even on various proposals by labelling them 'pastoral', the majority at the Council played both meanings of the term. The result is a paper agreement, not necessarily a substantial one.

Similar conclusions can be drawn from the diplomatic wording of many of the more disputed issues when they were finally set down in a Council document. A paper agreement was reached, but substantive differences remained.

By the conclusion of the Council there were definite expectations that the renewed Code would implement the reforms of the Council and even carry on the spirit of Vatican II. Given the divisions which are part of that spirit, it could be expected that the Code revision process would not be an easy one. Unconvinced in substance, the minority at the Council could look to the revision of the Code as a way to 'correct' what they might view as aberrations or excesses of the full assembly. The majority, on the other hand, had legitimate expectations based on Pope John's initial project and Pope Paul's continuing reference to it, that the new Code would crown the reform efforts whose main guidelines had been laid down by the Council.

(c) The next opportunity bishops had to express expectations about the new Code came at the first meeting of the World Synod of Bishops in October 1967. The meeting suffered from inadequate procedure and uncertainty on the part of many bishops as to their exact rôle and freedom to speak out. It also gave only a brief period of time for each of the five major topics on the agenda, and lacked mechanisms for Synod fathers to draft and debate proposals of their own.

There are two ways to read the bishops' expectations on the direction to be taken in the new Code from this Synod. A set of ten principles were presented, formulated in rather general and rambling terms by the Commission for the Revision of the Code.[23] After debate and à response by Cardinal Felici to the major observations, a sounding of opinion was taken according to the Vatican II formula for votes (*placet* and *non-placet* for yes or no votes respectively, and *placet iuxta modum* for reservations; these had to be submitted in writing). Each of the ten principles received a two-thirds approval, since reservations are counted as affirmative, but there were many *modi*. Nevertheless, it can be said the synodal fathers approved the direction proposed in the principles.

A less serene reading comes from an examination of the individual interventions of major figures at the Synod. Cardinals Urbani, Döpfner, Lefebvre, and Suenens, together with Synod members from some Third World and Eastern Catholic churches raised significant objections to elements contained in the principles, particularly as these related to the achievements of Vatican II.[24]

For example, the introduction to the principles explained the 1917 Code would serve as guide, the Council would furnish various *lineamenta*. Cardinal Urbani objected that what is needed is not simply a revision or even updating of the Code, but a genuinely new Code based on conciliar documents.[25] Cardinal Lefebvre echoed this position, calling for a Code which will be an attractive sign for all, both inside and outside the Church.[26] Cardinal Rossi urged involvement of a wider spectrum of people from around the world and various disciplines.[27] Cardinal Döpfner even offered two additional 'principles': that ecumenism have a more creative impact on the revision, and that laity be involved in further developing their own standing in canon law.[28] The appropriateness of law in the Church was affirmed by the Synod fathers but several speakers tried to balance a new juridicism by recalling the basic law for Christians is the gospel.[29]

Since many of these points were not directly in the ten principles they did not find expression in a final document of the Synod. Instead of amending the principles, a compilation of the *modi* was drafted by three Synod fathers and forwarded to the Code Commission. It has no binding force.

4. EXPECTATIONS AND RESULTS

It is clear the revision of the Code was designed to implement the decrees and spirit of Vatican II, to bring the renewal of the Church to bear on its institutional structures. From this perspective, the work to date is a mixed product.

The Code has been reorganised to conform to Vatican II categories. Sections of the law have been revised to incorporate various conciliar and post-conciliar directives. In spots it appears to be a welcome improvement. But clearly the 1917 Code and special legal theories have been more important than the Council in dealing with rights in the Church, distinctions of clerical status, and procedural law.

Canon law is not found only in a document. Political considerations of what is possible are as important as the text. A new Code will depend as much on the politics of its acceptance and implementation as on the expectations which shaped its drafting.

Notes

1. John XXIII, Solemn Allocution to Cardinals in Rome, 25 January 1959: *AAS* 51 (1959) 65-69.

2. P. Card. Felici, Report to the Synod of Bishops, 21 October 1980.

3. Benedict XV, *motu proprio* 'Cum iuris canonici', 15 September 1917; see S, Kuttner 'The Code of Canon Law in Historical Perspective' *The Jurist* 28 (1968) 129-148.

4. G. Hanlon *De Codicis Iuris Canonici Recognitione* (Rome 1964); P. Huizing 'Bulletin: The Reform of Canon Law' *Concilium* 8 (October 1965).

5. Kuttner, this article cited in note 3, 139-146.

6. John XXIII, the allocution cited in note 1, 68-69; *idem.*, Encyclical Letter 'Ad Petri Cathedram' 29 June 1959: *AAS* 51 (1959) 498.

7. Pope John repeatedly linked Synod, Council, and Code in at least twelve speeches and documents at a time when the process to revise the Code had yet to begin: *Periodica* 49 (1960) 67-141; 50 (1960) 44-135; 51 (1962) 48-118, 466-546.

8. D. Card. Tardini, Consultatio (TV interview), 24 January 1960: *Periodica* 50 (1961) 63.

9. F. Morrisey 'The Spirit of Canon Law, Teaching of Pope Paul VI' *Origins* 8 (1978) 34-40.

10. Paul VI, Allocution at Public Session of Vatican II on 18 November 1965: *AAS* 57 (1965) 983.

11. Paul VI, Allocution to Roman Rota, 4 February 1977: *AAS* 69 (1977) 148.

12. Paul VI, Allocution to Code Commission, 20 November 1965: *AAS* 57 (1965) 988.

13. Paul VI, Allocution to International Congress of Canon Lawyers, 25 May 1968: *AAS* 60 (1968) 337.

14. Y. Congar *Vraie et fausse réforme dans l'Église* (Paris ²1968) pp. 177-178; J. Provost 'Canon Law—True or False Reform in the Church?' *The Jurist* 38 (1978) 257-267.

15. *Acta et Documenta Concilii . . . Apparando*, Series I, Appendix Vol. II, 2 tomes (Vatican City 1961).

16. *Ibid.* tome 1, 235-239.

17. *Acta Synodalia . . . Vaticani II*, Vol. II, Pars IV (Vatican City 1972) pp. 771-826.

18. *Ibid.* pp. 382-392.

19. *Acta Synodalia . . . Vaticani II*, Vol. I, Pars IV (Vatican City 1971) pp. 142-144.

20. There was a general mood of optimism in much of the literature published about the Council at the time it concluded. For a more insightful commentary see E. Schillebeeckx *The Real Achievement of Vatican II* (New York 1967).

21. G. Philips 'Deux tendances dans la théologie contemporaine' *Nouvelle Revue Théologique* 85 (1963) 225-238.

22. Schillebeeckx, the book cited in note 20, pp. 84-85. He notes the significance of these approaches in the reform of canon law (at p. 87).

23. Pontificia Commissio Codici Iuris Canonici Recognoscendo, Principia quae codicis iuris canonici recognitionem dirigant, *Communicationes* 1 (1969) 77-100.

24. R. Laurentin *Le Premier Synode: Histoire et bilan* (Paris 1968) pp. 74-91.
25. G. Caprile *Il Sinodo dei Vescovi. Prima Assemblea Generale* (Rome 1968) pp. 95-96.
26. *Ibid.* pp. 96-97.
27. *Ibid.* pp. 99-100.
28. *Ibid.* pp. 106-107.
29. Laurentin, the work cited in note 24, at p. 80.

Ruud Huysmans

Canon Lawyers' Criticism
of the Drafts of the New Papal Law

THIS ARTICLE is of necessity very limited in its scope. In it, I shall not comment directly on the fundamental law of the Church or the law of matrimony, for example, nor shall I consider any theological, ecumenical or technical legal questions. I am, above all, concerned with developments in the Church's law that affect most believers directly. I shall consequently deal less with the considerable praise that the drafts of the new canon law have received from canon lawyers than with their critical reactions. The reader should bear this in mind. I have, after all, had to make a choice. In addition to various publications by individual canonists, I have also studied the collective commentaries made by German- and English-speaking canon lawyers. This has also imposed a limitation. Generally speaking, American canon lawyers have been harsher in their comments than those working in the Federal Republic of Germany. Not everyone who reads this article will feel able to agree with the views expressed here, but that is inevitable in such a summary.

1. PUBLIC CONFUSION

On 28 March 1963, Pope John XXIII appointed a papal commission to revise the *Codex Iuris Canonici* of the Latin Church. The name given to this commission pointed to its limited task, but, in the years that followed, it became clear from addresses made by Pope Paul VI and the president of the commission that the task would be much greater. It was not simply to be a question of improving the Codex—the commission had the task of reformulating the whole of the Church's law in the light of Vatican II and the new needs experienced in different countries and cultures. This gave rise to a serious dilemma—should there be a merely technical adaptation or should the law be fundamentally renewed? An important part was also played by the question concerning the extent to which the Codex of 1917 could provide a useful point of departure.

In 1965, it was decided to work at a 'fundamental law' that would apply to the whole Catholic Church. Since that time, however, it has never been entirely clear what this law should be. Should it state fundamental theological principles of Catholic ecclesiology, should it define the divine law of the structure of the Church, should it contain time-honoured and tested legal rules or should it consist of a selection of structures

10

common to both the Eastern and the Latin churches? The basic dilemma was between rules of law and statements about faith and there was also the lasting problem of the relationship between this fundamental law and the new Codex. Ever since the project was first launched, the degree to which the principle of subsidiarity ought to apply in the formation of the new law has never been quite clear. Did the papal legislator simply want to establish a few general principles and leave the conferences of bishops and individual bishops to a great extent free to make laws for their own territories or not? The consequence of this has been a dilemma between a detailed criticism of the drafts or a plea that the local churches should have legislative power.

In 1967, the First Synod of Bishops, which met at Rome, accepted with a clear majority a number of 'principles that should lead to the revision of the *Codex Iuris Canonici*', which were generally speaking given a positive reception. It became less and less clear, however, in the years that followed, when canon law was being revised, whether these principles still applied and, if so, to what extent. Finally, there was continuing confusion with regard to the primary aim of the revision of the law. Some canonists aimed at an adaptation of the hierarchical structure of the Church, while others tried to develop a code that would safeguard the freedom and the task of Christians. To what should attention be paid in particular? The sensitive nature of the legal patterns in different countries also contributed to this confusion.

2. A WAY OF APPROACHING THE PROBLEM

The rule of law—or canon—has power to organise functions that are regarded as socially important in a society and, with a predictable conflict in mind, to safeguard these functions in advance. The functions in question are those which would be too weak or too vague if they were not protected by the law. Canonists were given ample opportunity by the Second Vatican Council (1962-1965) and after the Council to study those cases in which functions that were already legally recognised needed to be adapted in comparison with the Codex of 1917 and those cases in which the law had to set up new functions and safeguard them. Canonists had also to look at the drafts that were circulated, through official or unofficial channels, between 1971 and 1977. Questions of the technique and systematisation of canon law played a part here and a great deal of attention was also given to old and new functions that were socially important in the light of the Church's life and mission. The universal Church had also in future to be seen as living in and from local churches. It is useful to group these functions under a number of different headings in order to classify the criticism of the various drafts to some extent.

3. EFFECTIVE LEGAL PROTECTION

It has always been accepted in the long tradition of the Church that a rule of law must play an important part in enabling just relationships to prevail in the life of the Church. Present-day canon lawyers have become very open to this important datum, partly under the influence of the human rights movement, an increasing knowledge of Anglo-Saxon legal traditions and various historical studies. It is therefore very regrettable that the fundamental rights of Christians have until now been formulated in such a limited and even vague way that they have only a very minimal significance in fact and provide too weak a foundation for legal protection. Another factor is that liability to punishment is regulated by canon law. One problem which has not yet been solved is whether canon law should not accept the principle of 'no crime and no punishment without the law' and not simply the weakened form of this in the draft.

The draft of the Church's penal law has also given rise to many serious questions. Should the hierarchy, for example, be given wide penal powers that are independent of any legal penal procedure? Should the power of the Church's leaders to decide whether or not to impose a punishment not be limited in order to prevent arbitrary decisions? Ought there not to be a much clearer definition of a number of fundamental notions and offences in the draft? Are there not too many penalties *latae sententiae*, which are automatic in their operation and therefore neither effective nor legally secure? Should it not be necessary to prove any assumption of culpability in external breaches of the law? A lack of responsibility on the part of those in authority in the Church and a negligent attitude on the part of clergy and laity in the service of the Church cause more harm than the faulty behaviour of ordinary believers. Ought the Church's law therefore not to give more attention to culpability of those in authority rather than to the question whether lay people, ordinary priests and religious should be punished? Should there not be a disciplinary law for persons in the service of the Church? Finally, surely automatic excommunication because of heresy, schism and loss of faith ought to be more clearly defined in order to protect the Church?

There is general satisfaction with the draft and especially with its attempt to regulate appeals made to the supreme hierarchical authority in administrative procedure with regard to decisions made by the Church's leaders. Generally speaking, however, there would seem to be a greater tendency in the Church for decisions regarding believers, both where the Church's penal law and where their opinions about Christian teaching and behaviour are concerned, to be made by the hierarchy than for such questions to be settled by means of legal proceedings. There is also the practical problem of the selection of suitable persons to serve in tribunals and courts. Finally, the procedure that has been suggested to deal with the forcible dismissal or transfer of parish clergy makes too little provision for the protection of the interests of the priest concerned.

4. THE GREATEST POSSIBLE PARTICIPATION OF ALL BELIEVERS IN THE LIFE AND MISSION
OF THE CHURCH

This claim is based on the idea of the Church as the people of God, possessing a common priesthood of all believers and receiving many gifts from the Holy Spirit. It is also based on the need for evangelisation, which is difficult to carry out in many countries. The Church's law has the task not only of not unnecessarily excluding many people and groups from the life and mission of the Church, but also of protecting and encouraging them to take part.

What is most regrettable in this context is that the task of the Church is regarded as that of the hierarchy. The task of teaching in the Church is, for example, almost exclusively that of the pope, the bishops and the priests. The exercise of the common priesthood seems frequently to be derived from and dependent on that of the hierarchy. This is clear evidence of an unacceptable ecclesiology. In this context too, it is noticeable that the rights of ordinary believers to take initiatives with regard to the apostolate are very limited and often vaguely defined.

The following more concrete points are also criticised in this context. Why, for example, can those in authority in female religious orders not be members of the Synod of Bishops? Why do married women necessarily have to have the domicile of their husbands? Why are women excluded from the new ministries? Why can they not act as judges, counsels for the defence of the marriage bond or *promotor iustitiae*? In addition to this, it is worth recalling that canon lawyers do not agree about the correctness of the principle that lay people can be ecclesiastical judges.

Why are the possibilities open to priests who have received a dispensation to marry fewer than those open to the laity? Is not too little account taken in the drafts of the fact that more and more tasks are now carried out in the Church and especially in pastoral work by lay people? Should no attention be given in the Church's law to their training and should almost exclusive attention continue to be given to the seminaries?

Most of the sacraments are described in the draft as an action taking place between the minister and the recipient. Why does the Church's law not insist, as the new *Ordines Romani* do, that the sacraments are to be celebrations of the people of God in the local community? Does the impediment of mixed marriage, especially between members of different churches, have to be retained? Should the number of impediments not, in general, be reduced? Can there not be more provision for collective absolution than there is in the present draft?

The exclusion of Catholics from the sacraments is a matter of great priority. At the same time, the suggestion that excommunicated Catholics should from now on be able to receive the sacraments of penance and the anointing of the sick is unacceptable in many quarters, since the connection between the person's inner life and his public life is broken by this practice. The proposed new canon law also no longer contains any provision for an explicit penalty against divorced and remarried Catholics. Like the law that is valid at present, there is also no special canon excluding them from holy communion. As a result, whether or not they should be excluded in all cases continues to be a question that is frequently discussed by pastoral workers, theologians and canon lawyers.

Two important criticisms have been made of the new law regarding declarations of invalidity of marriage. Should an ecclesiastical court not be declared competent on account of the domicile of the partner making the appeal and does the extended, formal and universal law of procedure, which has certainly been improved, really serve those who are asking for their marriage to be declared invalid? The point of departure for the application of this law is, after all, a legal dispute between two parties, but this is not always in accordance with the situation in which the parties find themselves, with the result that the procedure is often too slow and complicated. The procedure followed in declaring a marriage invalid ought therefore to correspond with the summary trial, which has now for the first time been proposed, or with the hearing for a dispensation because of a sexually unconsummated marriage. It is not so much a formal legal dispute as an attempt to discover the truth regarding a marital bond. There has also been some criticism of the need for the canon stipulating that the counsel for the defence of the marital bond must always give notice of an intention to appeal against a first declaration of invalidity.

Although there is widespread approval of the new law governing religious life in the Church because it is constructed according to acceptable principles, there have also been several serious criticisms. Should religious not be seen as living in communities rather than as institutes? Would this not lead to a different view of authority, implying that, in the case of female religious as well, superiors would be able to exercise full authority? Is it not artificial to attempt to deal with every type of communal life or following of the evangelical counsels in the Church in only one draft? Is degree of commitment to the apostolate a suitable criterion for arrangement? What, in other words, is more important in canon law—that the religious way of life should correspond to certain systematically arranged models that have been approved by the Church authorities or that the various forms of charismatic and associative life in the Church should be appreciated and protected? The legal relationships between the dioceses and religious communities appear in a very unfavourable light and this is mainly because of the considerable jurisdictional power enjoyed by the bishops with regard to the external activities of the religious.

This leads directly to the next criticism. In the draft 'On the People of God', there are proposals for various canons on associations of Christians, the clergy, the hierarchical constitution of the Church, religious and lay associations. Does this mean that there is ample recognition that, with the Church's mission in mind, there is a need for canons not only on the division of the Church into various communities that are entrusted to those in office, but also on communal initiatives taken by ordinary believers? The prospect that this will be realised would be better guaranteed from the legal point of view if the whole law of associations were considered under a separate heading rather than in small, scattered segments.

5. THE UNIVERSAL CHURCH NECESSARILY CONSISTS OF LOCAL CHURCHES

The insight was enunciated in principle during the Second Vatican Council. The local church is no longer primarily a hierarchical and territorial subdivision of the Church. It is a particular community of faith, entrusted to a bishop in co-operation with his priests. The bishop has all normal, direct authority in order to carry out his pastoral task, with the exception of certain reservations in the light of the pope's own task. There is therefore a source of authority in the local church by means of which that church can develop legitimately in its own way, but within the greater Catholic community, in which the bishops also have to represent their own church and therefore give prominence to what is authentic in its life.

The draft 'On the People of God' is especially worth considering in this context. The church in the diocese is only very poorly represented as an institution with the bishop in this document and it is to a great extent left to the bishop's discretion whether or not there is a diocesan pastoral council. The council of priests, the majority of whose members are not elected—only an appropriate part of this council has to be elected—only exceptionally has a decisive vote. The draft has nothing at all to say about parochial councils. The bishop's authority is recognised, but the reason for the papal reservations is not given. The bishop's authority to grant dispensations is limited to disciplinary laws, which 'have the spiritual good of the faithful directly in mind'. There is also no provision for any contribution to be made by the diocese in the appointment of a new bishop.

A two-fold division is made in this draft in the case of the 'hierarchical constitution of the Church'. On the one hand there is 'the highest authority of the whole Church and the exercise of that authority' and, on the other, 'the local churches and their associations'. The question arises here as to whether these associations between provinces and regions, at the middle level between the universal and the local church, should come under the heading of 'local churches'. What is at stake here is not only the original character of the local church, but also the special value of these episcopal associations, which have a part to play both in the government of the universal Church and in that of the separate dioceses. These associations are important because they can lead to a response by legislation and administration to the needs of the churches in their circle. The question that arises in this context is whether the episcopal conferences are not made too subject to Rome in the draft. According to the draft, Rome has to approve, both before and afterwards, all decisions made at regional councils, provincial councils and bishops' conferences. In addition, more provision is made in the drafts for legislative power in the case of episcopal conferences than in that of the various local councils. It is worth noting in this context that lay people and priests are permitted to take part in local councils as advisors, but that the episcopal conferences are closed assemblies.

The Synod of Bishops is described more as a help for the pope than as an expression of common concern. Its possibly decisive authority is seen by the draft as functioning relatively exceptionally. The Roman Curia was, according to the Second Vatican Council, at the service of the bishops, but this suggestion does not appear in any of the canons of the draft, which make it clear that it is at the service of the pope.

There is no provision in the 1976 version of the fundamental law of the Church for the pope's approval and free acceptance of collective action on the part of the scattered bishops, so that both pope and bishops can exercise their supreme collegial authority. There is only provision for an initiative to be taken by the pope. Canon lawyers are afraid that the new advisory organisations will be set up prematurely and will exist for a very long time because of the Church's new law. They are also afraid that there will be too great a distance, as a result of this new law, between the college of bishops, including and subject to the pope, and the individual bishops or the bishops in their various associations. The bishops and therefore the local churches are in danger of being too dependent on Rome.

6. THE HIERARCHICAL AUTHORITY OF ORDAINED OFFICE AS A SERVICE IN THE COMMUNITY

For canon lawyers, this is one of the most difficult spheres of all. If the gift of the Holy Spirit that is received at ordination is seen as an authority or power (*potestas*), this is clearly an interpretation made in the light of a definite legal tradition that was determined, at least partly, by Roman law. The fact that the idea of jurisdictional power has been replaced in the drafts by that of hierarchical power makes little difference to this. Some of the characteristics of this authority can be made clear in the following examples. The drafts require the bishop or priest not to recognise lay people as collaborators or advisers and not to work freely or publicly with any advisory bodies appointed. There is also no provision for any form of public accountability by the hierarchy in its government. There is no suggestion that the laity has any right to information about Church matters. In this way, a concept of public hierarchical authority that cannot be reconciled with such desires has implicitly continued. In addition to this, it is stated in the 1976 draft of the Church's fundamental law that the task of leadership in the Church regulates the legal and correct exercise of all the tasks in the Church. The only conclusion that can be drawn from this is that everything is subject to the authority of the hierarchy.

According to other drafts, this authority is invested in those who have received the sacrament of ordination. Most canon lawyers would agree with this, but it is certainly difficult to maintain in present circumstances, when there are too few priests for parish work and other tasks in the Church.

Authority in the Church, then, is reserved for bishops and priests and does not, in the legal sense, have to be exercised in collaboration with the community of believers. This means that, from the historical point of view, it can be exercised freely and without restriction. The really important critical question, however, is whether authority in this sense can be seen as a true service of the community. Will it not rather lead to the increasing isolation of the Church's hierarchy?

Translated by David Smith

Remigiusz Sobański

The Reform of the CIC—
A Polish View

1. THE PRE-CONCILIAR SUGGESTIONS AND REQUESTS

ON 18 June 1959 the president of the Preparatory Commission of the Council wrote to the future Council fathers to discover their views on the subjects to be discussed. Forty-three Polish bishops submitted their suggestions,[1] and they give us a picture of the expectations of Polish bishops associated with the Council.

The Polish bishops were in no doubt that the reformed law should retain the form of a Codex, but felt that the terminology needed standardising and that a new Codex should include both all intervening modifications and the clarifications resulting from authentic interpretation. One submission suggested that the laws of the Church and their official interpretation should be generally similar to civil laws, which would enable them to attain a more perfect form. The pastoral usefulness which a new Code should have was also stressed. The bishops wanted a number of canons deleted (984 n. 4, 987 n. 4, 1017, 1032 § 2, 1042 § 2, 1074, 1077 § 1, 1083, 1092) and suggested changes in others (88, 1076 § 2, 1083 § 2, 1096 § 1). It was felt desirable that new impediments to marriage should be introduced: ignorance about an incurable disease, chronic alcoholism and syphilis, when these were already present at the time the marriage was concluded, and discrepancy of blood groups. Simplification of the procedure for obtaining nullity and of the procedures of beatification and canonisation were demanded as matters of urgency. The importance of clerical dress was emphasised and the obligation to recite the breviary was insisted on, though there was generally a call for a reform or abbreviation of the breviary. Various prohibitions of a political nature were also suggested, and there was a call for a stricter enforcement of the spiritual exercises prescribed in can. 125. There were individual voices in favour of limiting the use (by clergy) of motor vehicles—and even of television—by canon law and also of forbidding attendance at the theatre and cinema. There was, however, also a call for priests to have greater contact with culture and art (Wojtyła).

It was generally felt by the Polish bishops that the position of the laity in the Church should be more precisely defined, and that this would enable them to take a greater part in the life of the Church. Even a Codex for the laity was proposed.

The wishes of Polish canonists were similar. The canon law faculty of the Catholic University of Lublin submitted observations on various provisions of the Codex together with a number of other proposals. The observations concerned Canons 66

16

(Incorporation of the quinquennial faculties into the Codex), 98 (equal status for different rites), 1035 (identical treatment for marital impediments leading to separation), 1042 (abolition of the minor marital impediments), 1083 (deletion of § 2, n. 2), 1087 (a time limit for a *purgatio metus*), 1429 (the fixing of the age at which abstinence becomes obligatory, and an obligation for all clergy to belong to a mutual aid association), 1432 (request for an administrative form for the conferral of pastoral offices). The following proposals were also submitted: the establishment of associations of priests to foster community life, a ban on any form of political activity by priests, a reform of the breviary, the simplification of clerical dress, the introduction of a minimum age of 28 for admission to the presbyterate and for solemn profession, easier release from the clerical state and the establishment in the seat of every metropolitan of an institute granting licentiates in theology.

2. THE PASTORAL BACKGROUND

This rapid survey of the proposals officially submitted to the future Council reveals the soil out of which they came. This was composed of (1) a definite ecclesial awareness, which was also highly influential in the first draft of the constitution on the Church, and (2) a specific pastoral and political situation.

With regard to the pre-conciliar sense of identity in the Church, it must be remembered that Vatican II far exceeded the expectations and ideas associated with it. This fact inevitably affected canon law—not just various institutions, but especially the theory of canon law. Polish canon law studies can show publications from the 1960s onwards which did not stay within the framework of traditional exegesis and historical scholarship but opened up fundamental areas of discussion about the nature of canon law. The need for a new approach to the fundamentals of canon law was stimulated in Poland not so much by the anti-juridical trend, which did not emerge with as much force here as in the West, but by the confrontation of ecclesiastical disciplines with religious studies, which were strongly secular in character and vigorously promoted. This situation forced a discussion of the specific features of theological knowledge and led to reflection on the nature of canon law.[2] The ecclesiology of Vatican II created an opportunity here. In the first reform of the Codex there will still be little trace of the influence of the discussions on legal theory initiated after the last Council. The time for a theologically based and matured codification has probably not yet come.[3]

Ecclesial awareness must be seen in the context of the specific pastoral situation, since this is the main influence on juridical ideas. For example, in the situation of the Church in Poland the unity of the Church was regarded, not just as one of its theological features, but as a vital necessity in the current state of relations between Church and State. The result was that great importance was attached to discipline, far beyond internal Church affairs. It is in this context that the suggestions about the rights of the laity in the Church should be seen; these were prompted by the desire to make them more active, but also to bind them more tightly to ecclesiastical discipline. One effect of the pastoral situation is that not only the hierarchy but also the laity look at canon law not merely in terms of the internal affairs of the Church, but also as relevant to their presence and effectiveness in their political environment.

The pastoral and political situation gives canon law a further rôle in the Church's dealings with the world beyond it. It is well known that law can and should be a stimulus to action. In particular canon law may be expected to promote exchange and evaluation of the experience of particular churches within the *communio ecclesiarum*. Whether or not the new codification leads to the chances of a revival in the life of the Church revealed by Vatican II being seized, and whether or not individual local churches are prepared to accept the new law as an invigorating force and to interpret it in this way, canon law is particularly valuable in many countries as a means of stimulating the life of the Church. An appeal to general canon law makes it easier to introduce locally new forms of pastoral work and Church activity.

Equally it should not be forgotten that the specific situation of the Church also encourages the development of particular law. This both helps to preserve traditional, tried forms of pastoral work and contributes to the development of privileged institutions.[4]

3. LAW IN THE LIFE OF THE CHURCH

This background explains why law should be accorded such great importance in the life of the Church in Poland, and why law was given so much attention in the bishops' submissions. Historical circumstances, which go a long way back into the past and are connected with the situation of the Church during the division of Poland in the nineteenth century, meant that canon law in Poland occupied a much more important position among the ecclesiastical disciplines than in other countries. Two faculties of canon law, Lublin and Warsaw, organised in conformity with the 1917 regulations of the Congregation of Studies, trained generations of canon lawyers in the spirit of 'curial' canon law who then served the Church by interpreting its laws according to the rules of can. 18 and also helped it to formulate clearly Catholic principles on the relationship of Church and State.[5]

If we add to the factors previously mentioned a relatively high identification of the faithful with the Church and a largely complete acceptance of the Council (which does not exclude a deviant interpretation), we have an adequate basis for summarising the expectations associated with the new canon law. It is seen as aid to integration (on a basis of disciplinary cohesiveness) and to promoting activity (in fixed channels). Because this integrating and activating rôle is regarded as an essential feature of the law, the announcement of the reform of canon law was welcomed. It was felt to be necessary, not because of any general critical attitude towards the Codex, but as a logical consequence of the Council.

For that reason the acceptance of the Council went hand in hand with the acceptance of the post-conciliar canon law. It was publicised and commented on as it appeared. Canonists objected to the form of the laws, which often left much to be desired from the legal point of view, but it was not criticised as incoherent. The only objections of substance expressed were to the weakening of the legal position of the parish priest in relation to the bishop. The impression of uncertainty in the law during the work of reform was avoided. The extent of the work of drafting, the often clearly provisional character of the laws promulgated and even the conviction that a great deal in canon law is out of date did not shake interest in the law of the Church in Poland. Demand for original texts and manuals in the field of canon law far exceeded the possible supply. From 1968 the faculty of canon law in the Academy of Catholic Theology in Warsaw published a collection of post-conciliar canon law: up to 1980 eleven volumes had appeared, each in three fascicules. This went out of print no less quickly than the manuals published by the same faculty, one in four volumes (fifteen fascicules) for specialists and one in two volumes for the clergy by E. Sztafrowski. In addition to these general works, manuals for such areas as marriage law and the law on religious orders were produced which, although going through several impressions, are today impossible to find. The editions are of course not that large, but the interest in the state of law in the Church is nonetheless clear.

The renewed Codex is awaited as the crown—and the conclusion—of the post-conciliar development of canon law. With the exception of a few theorists, who fear that in the current state of scholarship it will be lacking in theological maturity, one can say that there is a general desire for a new Code. Clergy want to have once more the whole of the law in force included in a convenient Codex. Canonists look to it as the natural fruit of the development of canon law. The hierarchy see it as the implementation of the principles of reform accepted by the 1967 Episcopal Synod. Lastly, the faithful, who daily come into contact with the flood of State legislation, see it as logical that, after a Council so concerned with ecclesiology, the Church too needs to alter its law. The faithful seem to put great faith in the expected Code.

On the other hand discussion about the reform is almost non-existent outside professional circles. It would be hard to find an article on the reform in Polish theological writing which was not written by a canonist. The Commission on the Reform of the Code set up in 1966 by the Polish Bishops' Conference is a further sign of this: it was composed of roughly half bishops (usually canon lawyers by training) and half canon lawyers.

The above remarks are certainly fragmentary. They are not intended as premises in a diagnosis, but give grounds for the belief that the introduction of the new Codex will encounter no serious difficulties in Poland. Its practical effectiveness remains to be seen.

Translated by Francis McDonagh

Notes

1. *Acta et documenta Concilio Oecumenico Vaticano II apparando* (Vatican City 1960) s. I, v. II, p. II, 643-776.

2. R. Sobański 'Note sulla questione della collocazione scientifica della canonistica, Strumento per un lavoro teologico' *Communio* 36 (1977) 70-81.

3. H. Schmitz *Auf der Suche nach einem neuen Kirchenrecht. Die Entwicklung von 1959 bis 1978* (Freiburg, Basle, Vienna 1979) p. 94.

4. The Polish Bishops' Conference can be taken as an example. J. Manzanarez, 'Las Conferencias Episcopales en tiempos de Pio XI (Un capitolo inedito y decesivo de su historia)' *Revista espan. de Derecho can.* 36 (1980) 12ff. A collection of Polish special law was published by the Academy of Catholic Theology in Warsaw, *Prawodawstwo Kościoła w Polsce 1961-1970*, oprac. T. Pieronek, I-II 1-3 (Warsaw 1971-74).

5. The importance of canon law within ecclesiastical disciplines has been remarked in discussion of Polish bibliographies: M. Zimmermann *Documentation, ordinateur et communautés chrétiennes* (Strasbourg 1973) p. 249 (*RIC* 1).

Joseph Khoury

The Election of Bishops in the Eastern Churches

INTRODUCTION

THE ELECTION of bishops has been a matter of the first importance in the life of the Church from earliest times. The bishop, the successor of the apostles, has always been the head of his eparchy, holding all powers and summing them up in his person, by virtue of his sacramental consecration and hierarchical communion with the head and members of the episcopal body.[1] The ways of choosing the person to exercise the episcopal rôle have nonetheless varied throughout the history of both the Eastern Churches and the Latin Church.

The aim of this essay is, first, to show how election has evolved in the history of the Eastern Churches, then to examine the present legislation on the subject contained in the *Motu proprio 'Cleri sanctitati'* of 1957, and finally to make some observations on the draft legislation now being considered.[2]

1. THE ELECTION OF BISHOPS IN OLD COMMON LAW

The Eastern Churches conformed to the norms laid down for the election of bishops by the Eastern councils from the first half of the fourth century. At that time, bishops were installed by the episcopal college of each province. The Council of Nicea (325) declared that 'it is most expedient that the bishop should be ordained by all the bishops of the province. If this is difficult, by reason of any pressing need or the great distances involved, then at least three bishops should come together and the others should have voted and made their opinion known in writing; the ordination should then proceed, and confirmation of what has been done in each province should be conveyed to the metropolitan'.[3]

The same Council also decreed: 'And let this be made clear to all: if anyone is made bishop contrary to the view of the metropolitan, this great synod declares that this candidate is not to be considered as a bishop. But if the candidate has been selected by common and reasonable decision and in accordance with ecclesiastical law, and two or three object on personal grounds, the majority opinion is to prevail'.[4]

The same rules were repeated by the Councils of Antioch and Laodicea, the Second Council of Nicea and the Council of Carthage.[5] The Eighth Ecumenical Council expressedly reserved the right of election to the episcopal college alone, excluding the participation of lay people, whether notables or princes, unless they had been invited by the College of Bishops.[6]

As a result of these laws of the early Eastern Churches, before the formation of the new patriarchates of the Uniates and the holding of their respective synods, bishops were elected by the provincial synod of bishops through a majority vote, taking the wishes of the Christian people into account. The metropolitan, the chief bishop of the province, verified the election and consecration procedures and was the intermediary through whom the newly-elected bishop was in communion with the See of Peter.[7] When the modern patriarchates were formed, the metropolitan had to obtain the consent of the patriarch before confirming the appointment.[8] Intervention on the part of the pope was occasional and generally confined to an election procedure tainted with irregularity.

1. THE ELECTION OF BISHOPS IN THE
INDIVIDUAL LAWS OF THE PATRIARCHAL EASTERN CHURCHES

The Maronite Church

In its constant fidelity to the See of Peter and its strictly patriarchal structure, the Maronite Church has managed to keep most closely to the old tradition for electing Eastern bishops. The choice was made by the patriarch operating with his synod and consulting eminent figures in the community. Following ancient custom, the people were given names in advance, and, unless there were serious objections, a choice was made from among candidates they approved.[9] This procedure was codified by the Council of Lebanon (1736), approved 'in forma speciali', and did not require any confirmation by the Holy See.

The Melkite Church

This too has remained faithful to the old traditions governing the election of bishops according to the rules laid down by the early councils of the East. Over the centuries, the election procedure developed in two significant ways, one in the eparchy of Aleppo and one in the others. In Aleppo, the choice was reserved to the secular clergy, who carried out the process in the presence of eminent citizens of the town, as witnesses to the proper course of the election. The result of this deliberation was passed to the patriarch, who checked that there was no canonical objection to the consecration by consulting the bishops of his Church. After consecration, the patriarch gave the newly-elected bishop the bull of jurisdiction over Aleppo.

In the other eparchies, the patriarch initially proposed three names chosen by him to the suffragan bishops. The bishops approved the list by majority vote, then the list was given to the secular clergy who had to choose a new bishop in the presence of eminent members of the community.[10]

In both cases, if after two scrutinies the electors had still not been able to agree on a choice, the election was remitted to the patriarch.[11]

The Holy See played no part in these elections either. 'The Melkite Synod', Mgr Edelby has written, 'has always had a free hand in the election of bishops, without being bound by any prior notification to, or subsequent confirmation by, the Roman Holy See. Out of deference to the Supreme Pontiff, the patriarch informed Rome simply of the name of the bishop.'[12]

C

The Armenian Church

The Armenian Synod, under the presidency of its patriarch, chose new bishops from among the candidates presented by the clergy and people of the vacant see.[13] This procedure was modified by the constitution *Reversurus* (1867), which required candidates to be presented, not by the clergy and people any longer, but only by the patriarch and the bishops assembled in synod, and the choice of the new bishop to be made by the Sovereign Pontiff.[14]

These new prescriptions were not accepted by all the Armenian clergy. Rome was forced to revise the bull *Reversurus* and modify the new procedure. By Decree of Propaganda of 6 December 1876, it was established that the patriarchal synod should make the choice, with the pope reserving the right to confirm it. The patriarch was also accorded the faculty of giving the newly-elected bishop, after his consecration, the canonical institution in the name of and by the authority of the Sovereign Pontiff.[15]

The Chaldean Church

The Chaldean Synod of 1853 established that the election of a new bishop depended on the patriarch choosing from a list presented to him by the clergy and people, after seeking the advice of the other bishops. But Pius IX, after the bull *Reversurus* for the Armenians, published another, *Cum ecclesiastica disciplina*, for the Chaldeans, laying down the same rules as for the Armenians. The Patriarch Joseph Audo opposed it. The pope revised the principles and gave the same concessions as to the Armenians: that the patriarch with the bishops could choose whom they wished in synod, and submit the name to the Holy See for confirmation.[16]

The Syrian Church

The choice of a new bishop in the Syrian Church was made by the patriarch and his bishops confirming a single name submitted by the clergy and people of the vacant see. To extend their choice, the Synod of Charfee in 1854 required that at least three names be submitted. The synod of 1888 laid down the same rules: the clergy and distinguished citizens should put forward three names for the patriarch and his bishops to choose from in synod, with the pope subsequently confirming the election.[17]

The Coptic Church

In the bull *Christi Domini*, Leo XIII, while restoring the Patriarchate of Alexandria and the two bishoprics of Heropolis and Thebes, reserved to the Holy See the right to set up other sees and appoint a bishop to them. The Synod of Alexandria in 1898 gave the patriarch and the three constituted bishops the right to submit a list of three candidates from which the pope could choose the new bishop for a vacant see.[18]

3. ELECTION OF BISHOPS IN THE NON-PARTIARCHAL EASTERN CHURCHES

In the non-patriarchal Churches of Bulgaria, Ruthenia, Rumania, Italo-Albania, Malabar, Malankares, Ukraine and Ethopia, bishops are nominated directly by the Holy See.[19]

Before the new discipline promulgated by Pius XII in 1957 and thereafter common to all the Eastern Churches, the picture was as follows:

(a) In the Maronite and Melkite patriarchal Churches, election was made by the patriarchal synod. The name of the bishop was communicated to the Holy See by the patriarch. It was only under Benedict XV that Rome began to publish in the *AAS* that the Holy Father '*ratam habuit*' this election, i.e., that he recognised it as valid.[20]

(b) In the Armenian, Chaldean and Syrian Churches, the election of a bishop was made in synod and had to be confirmed by the pope.

(c) In the non-patriarchal Churches, the appointment of bishops was reserved to the Holy See.

(d) In all the Eastern Churches the decision was a synodal, collegiate one, without this diminishing the primacy of the patriarch. He it was who collected information about the candidates, presided at the synod and, in certain Churches, had the sole right to propose names.

(e) The participation of the community in the election of bishops can be seen in various forms in all the Eastern Churches. In the Melkite Church, the Synod of 1790 gave the clergy and people of the diocese of Aleppo the right to elect a new bishop, it being understood that their choice had to be approved by the patriarch and the rest of the bishops. In other dioceses, the rôle of the laity and clergy was more restricted, while still being recognised as that of electors in a real sense.[21] The Synod of Lebanon laid down that the future bishop should be agreed by the faithful of the vacant see. The people had first say in expressing a preference for a particular candidate to the patriarch. If the patriarch twice rejected the candidates put forward by the people, he in turn had to have his choice accepted by the people and clergy of the diocese before consecrating him.[22] In the Armenian and Chaldean Churches, the people and clergy were invited to submit a list of candidates to the synod when a see became vacant. The Synod of Charfee (1888) empowered the people to present a list of three candidates to the patriarch, from which the synod made the final choice.[23] In the Coptic Church, the laity and clergy played a purely consultative role.[24] In the Ukranian Church, the clergy and laity have never played any part in the election of their bishops. In Rumania, on the other hand, it was only the clergy who could suggest candidates to the Holy See. Under the Hapsburgs, the emperor reserved to himself the right to choose one candidate from the three names put forward by the clergy and to submit this name to the Holy See. This privilege was abrogated after the fall of the Hapsburg empire, but a Concordat of 1927 still gave the clergy the right to submit a list of three candidates to the Holy See when a bishop was to be elected to the metropolitan see.[25]

4. THE ELECTION OF BISHOPS ACCORDING TO THE MOTU PROPRIO *CLERI SANCTITATI*

The 1957 legislation was preceded by a '*de mandato SSmi*' dated 15 December 1951, addressed to the heads of all the Eastern Churches by the Congregation for Eastern Churches.[26] This made the part of the proposed code of Eastern canon law dealing with the election of bishops mandatory. The new discipline came into force immediately, but had to remain a code of conduct for the heads of the Eastern Churches till the promulgation of the *Motu proprio 'Cleri sanctitati'* on 2 June 1957.

The new legislation gave the Sovereign Pontiff the right freely to appoint bishops in all the Eastern rites; he also reserved the right to confirm appointments made canonically (can. 392) in the patriarchal synods according to the prescriptions of canons 252-4. Synodical election could be made by one of two methods:

1. *First method (can. 252-3)*

The patriarch collects information and documents relative to the candidates he will put forward to his bishops. He then convokes the synod of bishops which will proceed to elect a new bishop from among the candidates proposed. Immediately after the election, the patriarch refers to the Holy See, informing it of the result and seeking confirmation of the candidate elected. Meanwhile, he is not allowed to communicate the name to anyone else, not even to the person concerned. It is only after confirmation has come from the Holy See that the patriarch asks the person chosen if he will accept the bishopric. He then informs the Holy See and liaises with it to promulgate news of the election in Rome and locally.

This method is in line with the rules formerly governing the procedure in the Armenian, Chaldean and Syrian Churches. It is not without its disadvantages, however. If the Holy Father has grave doubts about the person elected, he could refuse to ratify the choice; this would discredit the patriarch and his synod. Furthermore, the person chosen could refuse the charge, in which case the pontifical approval would have gone for naught.

In order to circumvent these difficulties, the legislation proposed a second method.

2. *Second method (can. 254)*.

The patriarch and his synod draw up a list of candidates suitable to the episcopacy. This list is submitted to the Holy See for its *nihil obstat*, which in curial practice is only valid for six months. The synod meets and chooses one name from among the candidates. Immediately after the election, canon 254 allows the patriarch '*illico ad ulteriora procedi*'. This means that he can make the election public and even confer episcopal ordination without consulting the Holy See. But out of deference, the patriarchs have usually contacted Rome before publishing the result of elections.

If the bishops chose a candidate from outside the list approved by the Holy See, the procedures laid down in the first method were to be followed.

For some years the *Osservatore Romano*, which publishes the elections of Eastern bishops in its '*provvista della Chiesa*' section, has not used the expression 'confirmation' but the term 'assent'. This seems to detract from the prescription of canon 392.2, which foresaw the 'confirmation' of an election carried out.

The main disadvantage of this method is its double recourse to the Holy See before the election of a bishop can be published. This is caused by the need to inform the Holy Father of the result of an election of which he had already approved before making it public in the communications media.

In non-patriarchal Churches and non-patriarchal territories, the nomination of bishops is still reserved to the Holy See.

In general, the reform had the advantage of unifying the procedures for electing a bishop in the Eastern Churches and of emphasising the part played by the Holy Father in such an important matter and one so intimately linked to the primacy. But it did not give lay people of the Eastern Churches the voice they had before.

5. COUNCIL GUIDELINES AND REVISION OF *CLERI SANCTITATI*

Article 9 of the Council Decree on Eastern Churches, *Orientalium Ecclesiarum*, 'decrees that their rights and privileges should be re-established in accord with the ancient traditions of each Church and the decrees of the ecumenical synods.

The rights and privileges in question are those which flourished when East and West were in union, though they should be somewhat adapted to modern conditions.'

Among the rights to be restored to the patriarchs are those concerning the election of bishops which they enjoyed before '*cleri sanctitati*' and even before the recent synods of the united communities. These rights provide that: 'the designation of bishops is always by means of an election in the provincial synod presided over by the metropolitan, or in the patriarchal synod presided over by the patriarch, or in any other synod enjoying internal canonical autonomy'.[27]

After the Council decree was promulgated, the Melkite Church, in a letter to Paul VI, expressed its determination to elect new bishops, 'without being bound by the restrictive clauses of the (said) *Motu proprio*, with particular reference to the obligation to obtain approval from the Holy See of the list of possible candidates or of the election itself'.[28] The Melkite Church does not deny the inalienable right of the Holy Father to intervene in any particular case, but this does not involve an obligation to intervene, i.e., the exercise of this right.[29] In a reply addressed to Patriarch Maximos IV, (16 July 1965) the Secretariat of State made the following points: the intervention of Rome in episcopal elections has never been other than beneficial, defending the Eastern Churches against pressure from the civil power; Rome's confirmation of elections was requested by some of the Eastern Churches, not imposed by the popes; the Ecumenical Council itself declares that some adaptations must be made to modern conditions; it is inadvisable to deprive Rome of a certain discreet control, which has produced excellent results in the past. . . .[30]

The Melkite Church then suggested a 'practical procedure before the election, giving the patriarch, in his personal capacity, on the one hand, the chance to receive useful confidential information from Rome, and on the other hand giving the pope the opportunity of intervening, if he judges it necessary, either to name a candidate directly or rule one out by making use of his primatial right'.[31]

Through recourse to the 'Central Commission for co-ordinating post-conciliar work and interpreting the decrees of the Council', the question was resolved by giving an authoritative interpretation of Article 9, by which: 'The patriarchs should put forward the names of candidates and wait for the Holy See to reply on their suitability. The patriarchs may also, following a very ancient custom, ask the Sovereign Pontiff for confirmation.' ·

Ivan Žužek finds the Melkite action (electing bishops without approval from Rome) quite in accord with Article 9 of the Decree, and the exchange of official letters between Rome and the Melkite patriarch indicates an application and interpretation of this article which will certainly influence future Eastern canon law.[32]

6. THE ELECTION OF BISHOPS IN THE SCHEMA FOR THE NEW CODE

The Commission considers the election of bishops a question of the highest importance for the Eastern Churches. The basic principles which have guided it in drawing up a new Code are the fruit, according to its secretary, Ivan Žužek, 'of long work of reflection and research based on very thorough reports on the procedures followed by the patriarchal synods before the Second Vatican Council established' the content of Article 9 of the Decree on Eastern Churches.[33]

These principles are: an effective collegiality which requires the greatest co-responsibility on the part of all the bishops of an Eastern Church; the establishment of a list of candidates; the possibility of choosing the new bishop from outside the list; the collection by bishops themselves and not just the patriarch (as in the *ius vigens* of canon 252) of information on the candidates they propose; discreet consultation not only with the '*presbyteri eparchiae vacantis*' but also with some lay people who excel '*prudentia et christiana vita*'.[34]

Once the information is collected, the patriarch always has the faculty to add to it if necessary, and then, '*rem ad omnes Synodi sodales transmittat*'. The synod meets, and votes for a list of possible candidates which the patriarch submits for the approval of the

Holy See. Once this is granted, with no time limit, the synod can proceed to the election in the established way.[35]

The synod can elect a candidate from the list previously communicated to the Holy See, or it can choose someone not previously selected. In the first case, the new legislation gives the patriarch the right to ask the person elected for his consent and then inform the Holy See of the result of the election, indicating the date when this should be published, in Rome and locally. This procedure gives practical value to the *'illico ad ulteriora procedi'* of canon 254 of *Cleri sanctitati*. In the second case, the patriarch informs the Holy See and asks for the Holy Father's approval; the result can only be announced, as provided for in canon 252, once the pope has given his assent.[36]

This procedure only applies to the patriarchal and major archiepiscopal Churches; in the others, episcopal nomination is still reserved to the Sovereign Pontiff.

For nominations outside the patriarchal territories, the patriarchs and their synods present a *terna* of candidates to the pope. This is in accordance with the rules laid down by the Congregation for the Eastern Churches in 1970.[37]

7. THE FUTURE

The new Code, which is of course not in its final form, is limited to putting the current discipline into practice, with the modifications indicated above. It is to be hoped that the adaptation of the rights and privileges of the patriarchs to modern conditions will be further elaborated and better defined.

For instance, the question of the 'right' of Eastern rite bishops to direct *communio* with the universal Pastor is a point requiring further consideration. For instance, could the Eastern Churches who asked Rome to confirm episcopal elections, as the Secretariat of State wrote to Patriarch Maximos IV, be said to have done so precisely because this seemed to them an expression of this *communio* brought about through the mediation of the patriarch?[38]

The new legislation points in the direction of more effective synodal collegiality. It would be useful to clarify the links that should exist between the patriarchal synod and the bishops of non-patriarchal territories. This is a problem of far greater magnitude than the election of bishops and its attendant juridical aspects. Finally, it would be desirable if the new legislation could find an effective way of making the voice of the laity heard in the election of bishops, while recognising that choice is one thing and consecration another.

Translated by Paul Burns

Notes

1. Decree on the Bishops' Pastoral Office in the Church, §4; Pius XII *Motu proprio 'Cleri sanctitati'* can. 392.
2. *Nuntia* (organ of the Commission for the revision of Eastern canon law) 9 (1979).
3. J. Gaudemet *Les Elections dans l'Eglise Latine des Origines au XVIme siècle* (Paris 1979) pp. 16-17; see also S. C. Orientali *Codificazione canonica orientale, Studi preparatori: can. 329-90 (de Episcopis)*.
4. Gaudemet, the article cited in note 3, at p. 17.
5. *Ibid.* pp. 17, 19.
6. See Mansi XVI col. 174-5.

7. G. Thils *Choisir les eveques? Elire le pape?* (Paris 1970).

8. A. Coussa *Epitome praelectionum de iure ecclesiastico orientale* (1948) I p. 291, nn. 387ff; see Assemani *B.O.* III, II p. 702; *Codex Liturg.* XIII p. 78.

9. Synod of Lebanon (1736), II, IV, 15; see I. Aouad *Le Droit privé des Maronites* (Paris 1933) p. 100.

10. C. Charon *Histoire des Patriarcats Melkites* III (Rome 1911) pp. 549-550.

11. *Ibid.*

12. N. Edelby *Les Eglises Orientales Catholiques* (Paris 1970) p. 363.

13. Charon, the article cited in note 10, at p. 559; see Mansi XL col. 810: Council of Bzommar (1851).

14. *Ibid.* p. 560; Coussa, the work cited in note 8, at p. 294; *Pius IX Pontificis Maximi Acta* 1, 4, 304-322; 1, 5, 38-47.

15. Charon, the work cited in note 10, at p. 562; Martinis, VI, 2, p. 367.

16. Charon, the work cited in note 10; see S. C. Orientale *Codificazione canonica orientale, Fonti*, Series II, fasc. XVII, 'The acts of the Chaldean Synod' p. 48.

17. Synod of Charfee (Rome ed.) pp. 223-225.

18. Charon, the work cited in note 10, at p. 563.

19. Charon, *ibid*; see *Codificazione. . . . Studi preparatori*, can. 271 'De patriarchis'; Coussa, the work cited in note 8, at p. 299.

20. Coussa, the work cited in note 8, at p. 298; see Edelby, the work cited in note 12, at p. 363.

21. Charon, the work cited in note 10, at p. 552.

22. Synod of Lebanon, II, IV, 15.

23. Charon, the work cited in note 10, at p. 552.

24. Coussa, the work cited in note 8, at p. 295.

25. M. M. Wojnar 'Participation of the clergy and laity in the election of bishops according to the discipline of the Oriental Catholic Churches' in *The Choosing of Bishops* (Connecticut 1971) pp. 61ff.

26. Edelby, the work cited in note 12, at p. 364.

27. *Ibid.* p. 362.

28. *Ibid.* p. 362.

29. *Ibid.* p. 360.

30. *Ibid.* p. 365.

31. *Ibid.* p. 366.

32. I. Žužek 'Opinions on the Future Structure of Oriental Canon Law' in *Concilium* 8, 3 (Oct. 1967) 65-75.

33. *Idem.* in *Nuntia* 9 (1979) pp. 3ff.

34. *Ibid.* p. 10.

35. *Ibid.* p. 11.

36. *Ibid.* p. 13.

37. Declaration of the S.C. for the Eastern Churches, in *AAS* 62 (1970) 179; see also *Nuntia* 6 (1978) p. 30.

38. W. de Vries 'The "College of Patriarchs"' in *Concilium* 1, 8 (Oct. 1965) 35-43.

Peter Lengsfeld

Revised Ecclesiastical Law—
An Ecumenical Viewpoint

'I'M NO expert in the field of canon law, but it seems to me that ecclesiastical law is a necessary instrument for realising the ecumene.' This statement by an Orthodox bishop[1] will also find agreement among ecclesiastical law experts and ecumenists, unless they intend practising *ecumene* in a legally irrelevant way or ecclesiastical law in an unecumenical way. For what the above-mentioned bishop then went on to state with regard to the schism between the Roman Catholic and the Eastern Church also holds for Western schisms: 'The great breach of 1054 between Rome and Byzantium was also a legal problem. And therefore ecclesiastical law should contribute to restoring unity.' In all fairness one cannot expect more than one contribution, but after over fifteen years of reform work on Catholic ecclesiastical law the question arises of whether the chance offered by any ecclesiastical reform of making a contribution to understanding and union among all Churches has in this case been used or thrown away. In the final analysis, the revision of ecclesiastical law in a Church which constitutes roughly half of all Christianity is not without significance for the other half of Christianity. And conversely, the interest and critical attention of the rest of Christianity in such a reform process cannot be without significance for the church which is reforming its law.

Even though a legal communion between the divided Churches, which might be viewed as a victory over divisions, is a long way off, and therefore legal obligations based on a *communio* of the Churches cannot yet be enforced, the ecumenical movement has nevertheless created or perhaps revealed a situation in which no Church can any longer undertake major developments in its law, its doctrine or its activities with regard to the outside world, without the smaller Churches being affected by it. In a certain spiritual and factual sense it must be said that the *communio, etsi non perfecta* of which the Decree on Ecumenism of the Second Vatican Council spoke, is already a reality. Important events in the ecumenical debate (e.g., agreement on baptism, Eucharist and office, the antiracism debate), in the Reformation Churches and Anglican community of churches (ordination of women, Leuenberg Concord) and the Eastern Churches (Panorthodox Council) are also significant for the Catholic Church; likewise the revision of Catholic ecclesiastical law is also of importance for the other Churches and communities. Anyone even faintly aware of the difficulties the Orthodox Churches have had in the preparation of their Council and the Reformation Churches in the formation of inter-regional liaison structures, could not help feeling a special interest in seeing how

28

a world-wide tradition-rich Church is trying to re-fashion its traditional law and to translate the impulses of the Council into a universally valid ecclesiastical code. There can be no doubt of the ecumenical significance of the Codex reform—and ecumenical here has its literal meaning of concerning the whole of world Christianity.

ECHO AND CONCERN

Nevertheless, the general echo aroused by this plan of the Catholic Church has been comparatively faint. As Hans Dombois (Heidelberg), the most interconfessionally committed Protestant ecclesiastical law expert, was able to report,[2] Orthodox and Anglican representatives have collaborated in the papal commission, although without much success; the Reformation Churches, however, who were also invited, have, in spite of an additional recommendation of the Ecumenical Council, not accepted the Roman offer to send consultors. In his view the Reformation Churches have in this way also 'lost the moral right to continue to voice their criticisms, as at all times in the past, of the ecclesiastical law system of the Catholic Church' (*ibid.*). This is much to be regretted. The responsible Roman Catholic Commission has missed out on essential impulses from the Reformation Churches, and the Reformation Churches for their part have been able neither to make their full contribution to Catholic reform, nor to profit from discussion of the problems of a world-wide Church which are also relevant for their own legal structure. A reciprocally interesting co-operation in the field of ecclesiastical law apparently exists so far only at the level of private initiatives or meetings of experts (e.g., in Austria, Germany and the USA), but not at the level of the world-wide Churches and confessional groups. This may be connected with a widespread allergy to ecclesiastical law as such. In fact, the relevance of the norms and provisions of ecclesiastical law to the gospel of Jesus Christ and what believing people have experienced and wish to construct together from the revelation of Jesus, is seldom clear. But many forget here too that both the experience and the possibilities of a way of life are dependent on the preconditions and structures laid down by ecclesiastical law. Participation in their construction, therefore, should actually be an important concern of all Christians and Christian experts interested in a reform of the legal framework for Christian life and in the community of witness for the Christian revelation of God. Therefore it is to be regretted from the points of view of both ecclesiastical law and ecumenism that concrete participation in the revision of Catholic ecclesiastical law has been so slight in all the Churches, even the Catholic, and that the general echo from the non-Catholic Churches has been almost totally lacking. Apart from the contributions, of which nothing in much detail is known, of the Orthodox and Anglican consultors at the Catholic Commission for the Reform of the *Codex Iuris Canonici*, probably only the Heidelberg work groups of Protestant and Catholic canonists, led by Hans Dombois, have been able to exercise a certain, if slight, influence on the final form of the revised Catholic ecclesiastical law. Their reaction to the first drafts of the *Lex Ecclesiae Fundamentalis* was able to include—not least because of the long-known commitment of Hans Dombois himself to ecumenical-ecclesiastical law—the concern of many non-Catholic Christians and ecumenists. Christians of all confessions who are ecumenically committed and interested in ecclesiastical law might have similar concerns, even though they do not label the whole draft forthwith an 'ecumenical offence'. They touch in particular on three fields:

(a) Baptism and church affiliation

In ecumenical circles strong objection was expressed to the legal notion taken over from the old CIC (can. 6 LEF 1971), with only minor alterations, into the *Lex Fundamentalis* (can. 6), according to which baptism, any baptism, even baptism performed in a non-Catholic Church, establishes *a priori* a fundamental legal relationship to the Roman Catholic Church. This meant that Protestant and Orthodox and other Christians, on the basis of their baptism, in principle were also subject to the legal jurisdiction of the Roman Catholic Church (see can. 12 of the old CIC), even though they had in fact no contact whatsoever with that Church and were not affected by the legal consequences of this fundamental incorporation. According to the well-known obex-theory (obex = obstacle, bar), affiliation to another Church was regarded only as an 'obstacle' and 'bar', as an impediment, in other words, which does not allow the normal legal consequences of baptism to ensue, although all non-Catholics, owing to the valid baptism, are in principle subject to the supreme legal power of the pope.

In this connection Wilhelm Steinmüller has pointed out[3] that the new draft law only cites preconciliar sources, 'although precisely these texts were the subject of the sharpest criticism at the Council'. It could certainly not have been easy to find a clear-cut and also ecumenically acceptable solution to this problem, for baptism has dogmatic and ecclesiastical-law dimensions, the latter of which includes both *ius divinum* and *ius mere ecclesiasticum*, and all these have to be harmonised with the recognised legitimacy of baptism in other Churches and communities. Since the Decree on Ecumenism of the Second Vatican Council it must be said that the legitimacy of baptism in other Churches can no longer—not even tacitly—be substantiated on the model of 'heretical baptism'; it is rather connected to the fact that the 'separated Churches and communities' are to be regarded as very 'means of salvation' (Section 3). This offered the chance to substantiate the legitimacy of baptism in the other Churches and church communities differently from former times, from the Catholic point of view. Recently a draft proposal for a revised version of can. 12 (*Normae generales*) was made known which, however, also seems unsatisfactory. According to it non-Catholic Christians are regarded by Catholic ecclesiastical law as 'not directly obligated' (*non directe obligati intelliguntur*). Such a formulation of course immediately raises questions, such as: are they in that case 'indirectly' obligated? Under what circumstances can a direct obligation ensue? And above all: Is the question of exemption from Catholic ecclesiastical law really only a question of 'view', i.e., of the manner in which the Catholic legislator 'considers' it (perhaps in the sense of a simulation?), or would the latter not in fact have to work out a formulation which avoids any subsumption of non-Catholic Christians under Catholic ecclesiastical law?

A proposal of the Heidelberg ecclesiastical law experts[4] states: 'Legibus mere ecclesiasticis non tenentur qui . . . non sunt baptizati in Ecclesia catholica . . .' (as new beginning of Art. 3 of can. 6).[5] That was at least a positive clarification which could replace the former legal fiction and render the obex-theory superfluous. Whether in any view it is enough in itself to dispel any doubts—e.g., with regard to the *ius divinum*—of course remains an open question. However the adoption of such a text, stemming from a highly regarded interconfessional group of experts, would be not only a sign of ecumenical co-operation, but also a contribution to the inner and outer credibility of Catholic ecclesiastical law where all non-Catholic Christians are concerned.

(b) Interconfessional marriages

It is precisely in the question of the law on membership that, for the sake of *ecumene*, a maximum of clarity must be striven for. Any unclarity here can have very practical consequences, e.g., in the law on mixed marriages and in discussions preceding the ceremony of an interconfessional marriage. Many older parish priests will still remember the difficulties when they had to explain to a non-Catholic spouse that the promises affected him or her too, and not just the Catholic spouse, and that this was lawful, indeed had to be demanded on the basis of *ius divinum*. Meanwhile non-Catholic Christianity has learned with some amazement 'that the paragraphs of divine law declared unrenounceable (for example the obligation to give children a Catholic education) were reduced in exegesis to what is possible for the individual ("quantum posse"), while in the application of the ecclesiastical, i.e., alterable, law, although the troublesome formal obligation is upheld, the main practical difficulties are however removed by rules of dispensation, etc.'.[6]

But independently of the clarification of the question of confessional affiliation in connection with baptism, and even after the revision of 1970 of the law on mixed marriages, there are still considerable problems, which the Codex legislator should take into consideration. The maintenance of the prohibition on mixed marriages even for such confessionally mixed regions as central Europe (and the USA, but also elsewhere), still represents from the ecumenical viewpoint a discrimination against non-Catholic Christianity. It also often has a discriminating effect on the Catholic spouse, who is regarded in his or her parish as a Catholic of inferior quality. Moreover the complicated administration of the formal obligation, which is also valid for mixed marriages, at the marriage ceremony, has led to the intolerable situation that in a region like the Federal Republic of Germany, every year about 70,000 Catholics enter into a marriage which is 'invalid' according to ecclesiastical law. To these are added about 23,000 mixed marriages contracted in Protestant churches, in which it was neglected to obtain ecclesiastical dispensation for the Catholic partner, so that these marriages too, according to Catholic ecclesiastical law, are 'invalid'. As the non-obtaining of the dispensation in most cases probably occurs not out of indifference to church application, but has its roots in the complicated nature and inexplicability of the law on dispensation itself, here too legislative tasks present themselves. If they are not solved by the time of the final version of the revised Codex, a great chance for the settlement of practical ecumenical problems will have been missed. The request for the abolition of the formal obligation (or at least for a general dispensation) put forward by the Protestant side on the occasion of the pope's visit to Germany should be seriously considered.

Since the representatives of the Protestant Church in Germany, in their discussion with the pope, pointed out the many still unsolved problems regarding mixed marriages, as was also publicly acknowledged, discussion on it will not die down so quickly. Perhaps solutions which are incontestable from the point of view of ecclesiastical law and meaningful from the pastoral point of view will not be possible at the level of the Church as a whole. Possibly, then, the problems of those countries which are so strongly mixed confessionally could be an important motive for differentiating more strongly between universal-church and local-church legislation.

(c) Church and Churches

The question of how the Catholic Church intends to articulate its self-image in the revised Codex has also attracted great attention. Here, has the self-image which emerged so fascinatingly during the Council in terms of the people of God on pilgrimage, as *communio* not only hierarchically ordered, but also fitted out at all levels with synodal bodies, as contrasted with the onesidedness of the concept of the *societas-(perfecta)*, been sufficiently expressed? Is the recognition of the equal value of non-Latin rites and local churches also been legally carried through? Is the collegiality between pope and bishops, between bishops and priests, and priests and laity being developed consistently? On the basis of the general priesthood of all believers, are the basic rights of the laity being extended, beyond former limits, to be able to receive the Word of God and the sacraments, in the sense of a living participation (*actuosa participatio!*) of all in that which concerns all? And above all: How is the self-image of the Catholic Church defined in relation to the other Christian Churches and Church communities, which the Council recognised—although imperfectly—as 'media salutis'?

According to what has become known so far of the revised Codex, the answer to all these questions, which are of great importance from the ecumenical viewpoint, emerges as unsatisfactory, not to say disappointing. The principle which was long emphasised by the Reformation Churches, but re-appropriated in the Decree on Ecumenism, of 'perennis reformatio', was indeed positively adopted (in can. 2 Art. 2(4) LEF 1971) and the obligation 'that all are one' cited in connection with it. But the fact that these concepts had a prominent place precisely in the Decree on Ecumenism and claim recognition in the ecumenical context, seems to have been completely forgotten by the authors of the new text of the law. For they relate them in the same section not to the relationship to the non-Catholic Churches, but to the inner-Catholic local churches, primarily the old patriarchal Churches, who are exhorted, with due regard for every legitimate difference in rites and customs, to preserve the unity of the faith and not to damage the unity of the (Roman Catholic) universal Church. The originally ecumenical connection, i.e., aiming at union with the divided Churches, between Church reform and reunion, inner-Catholic renewal and capacity for union with the divided Churches, no longer has any scope.

The most disappointing thing is the fact that wherever one's view is directed outwards, beyond the ecclesiastical-law limits of the Catholic Church, it appears, exactly as in pre-conciliar times, that only *individual* Christians can be affected. It is said of the *individuals* that they (can. 7, Art. 2 LEF 1971) belong to Churches or communities which are separated from the Catholic Church and nevertheless, on the basis of their baptism and their faith, stand in a certain, if not total, *communio* with the Catholic Church. They, the individual non-Catholic Christians, are said justly to bear the name Christian and are therefore recognised as 'brothers in the Lord'. For all Christians, Catholics and non-Catholics, who at the time saw in the Decree on Ecumenism ecumenically significant progress, the actual elimination of essential elements of this Decree must be a bitter disappointment. For if the decree on Ecumenism (Section 3) ascribes to other Christian Churches and communities significant elements which go to build up the Church, and therefore the Churches and communities are recognised as means of salvation which the spirit of Christ himself uses to bring salvation, then the ecclesiological status thereby dogmatically acknowledged may not be revoked again by ecclesiastical law. Such a reduction of non-Catholic Christianity must be interpreted as an anti-ecumenical act committed by a Church which links dogma and law at all levels more closely together than any other Christian church. No one feels more strongly estranged from his concrete interacting partner—and between the non-Catholic Churches and the Roman Catholic Church there have been meanwhile innumerable interactions, collaborative relations and dialogues—than someone whose already acknowledged status is disarmed again, indeed whose existence is suddenly no longer even acknowledged.

It would be very desirable if at least on this point a fresh revision of the revised Codex were carried out, so that dogmatics and law, ecumenical practice towards the outside world and ecumenical attitude within, do not diverge widely in the long term. One possibility of escaping from this dilemma would be the adoption of the Heidelberg proposal for a new text (instead of the former can. 2(4) LEF 1971), which does not damage the self-image of the Church in any way and yet gives expression to a positive recognition of ecumenical relations and obligations. The proposed text reads: 'The Catholic Church recognises a community, although not yet complete, between itself and other Churches and Church communities', and it recognises 'also, that it is bound, together with these, according to Christ's mission, to work towards full communion'.[7]

Without compromising itself, in this way the intentions of the Council, in particular the instructions of the Decree on Ecumenism and of the Ecumenical Directories and also of ecumenical reality, which has already developed since the Council, could then be responded to in a sense which would also be clearly recognisable for non-Catholic Christianity.

A final judgment from the ecumenical viewpoint is not yet possible, since many texts are not yet available in the final version. In the texts known until now at least three sensitive points of ecumenical significance have been handled unsatisfactorily, in a way which is inconsistent with regard to the Council, and disappointing. In 1971 Wilhelm Steinmüller called the then available (fourth) draft of the basic law 'the most massive obstacle . . . that, since the coming into force of the *Codex Iuris Canonici*, people have placed before the wish of the Lord "ut omnes unum" '.[8] Whether the new ecclesiastical law proves to be such a massive obstacle for the progress of ecumenical union, the future will show. The hope of the Orthodox bishop quoted at the beginning, that ecclesiastical law could be an 'instrument for realising *ecumene*', or at least 'contribute to restoring unity', does not in any case appear to be fulfilled. Will the next reform of the Codex take the ecumenical situation more fully into account and take advantage of the chances offered by the Council?

Translated by Della Couling

Notes

1. As reported by W. M. Plöchl 'Das Kirchenrecht im Dienste der Ökumene' *Österr. Archiv f. Kirchenrecht* 24 (1973) 18-29, 26.
2. H. Dombois *Kodex und Konkordie* (Stuttgart/Frankfurt 1972) p. 63.
3. W. Steinmüller 'Die Lex Ecclesiae Fundamentalis—Ein ökumenisches Ärgernis' *Stimmen d. Zeit* 188 (1971) 386-400, 392.
4. See P. Weber, H. Dombois, A. Hollberbach *Periodica de re morali, canonica, liturgica* 62 (1973) 423-466, 447.
5. The latest draft of the new CIC (1980) takes this wish into account in its c. 11(1), where it states: 'Legibus mere ecclesiasticis tenentur baptizati in Ecclesia catholica vel in eandem recepti . . .'.
6. H. Dombois *Kodex und Konkordie* p. 61.
7. *Ibid.* p. 36; and *Periodica*, cited in note 4, at p. 447.
8. W. Steinmüller, in the article cited in note 3, at p. 400.

PART II

Vatican II and the New Code

Joseph Komonchak

The Status of the Faithful in the Revised Code of Canon Law

AN EVALUATION of the status of the faithful in the new Code of Canon Law is complicated by the incomplete information so far available. In 1977 the Pontificial Commission for the Revision of the Code issued a *Schema Canonum Libri II De Populo Dei* (SDPD). This included a chapter on 'The Obligations and Rights of All the Faithful'. But the twenty-four canons of this chapter were extensively revised by the *Coetus De Populo Dei* in October 1979. Twenty of the canons were dropped either in whole or in part, on the grounds that their subjects would be included in a similar section of the proposed *Lex Ecclesiae Fundamentalis* (LEF). The latest version of this document, however, is not available and can only be reconstructed from the reports of the *Coetus* on the LEF, particularly that of the meeting of September 1979. The *Schema Codicis Iuris Canonici* (SCIC) sent to the Fathers of the Pontifical Commission in 1980 does not contain a section on common and fundamental rights and duties, this also apparently on the grounds that this material will be contained in the LEF. Since the LEF is still somewhat problematic and since the exact wording of the pertinent texts cannot be ascertained (the canons of the LEF and of the SDPD not always coinciding), an interpreter can only draw upon the reports of the two *Coetus* and then examine what concrete expression of rights and obligations is given in the SCIC.

A decision to include in the new Code a section on the common and fundamental rights and obligations of the faithful was already made in the 'Principles to Guide the Revision of the Code of Canon Law' which were presented to and endorsed by the 1967 Synod of Bishops. The sixth of these principles concerned the defence of the rights of persons. While asserting the authority of pope and bishops, the document noted that divine and ecclesiastical law prohibits its abuse:

> The rights of every Christian must be acknowledged and defended, both those which are contained in the natural and divine positive law and those which are fittingly derived from them on account of the social condition which the faithful acquire and possess in the Church.
>
> And since all do not have the same function in the Church nor possess the same status, it is rightly proposed that, because of the radical equality obtaining among all the faithful on account of their human dignity and the baptism they have received, in

the new Code a *juridical statute* common to all be elaborated before considering the rights and duties which belong to the various ecclesiastical functions.[1]

This principle had already been adopted by the *Coetus* on the Laity and Associations of the Faithful at its first meeting in 1966. While there was some disagreement noted on the notion and pertinence of 'subjective rights' in the Church, this was not considered to affect the general principle that provision must be made to state and defend the rights of the faithful:

> The *Coetus* considered that certain rights, faculties, and duties without doubt flow from the very condition of every baptised person, by virtue of the divine law itself, both positive and natural. This complex of rights and duties, since it is based on the divine law and is a radical exigency founded in the ontological condition of a Christian believer itself, exists prior to any positive law and has force independently of any such law. It is, however, fitting—and indeed necessary—that human law receive such rights and duties, state them clearly, and provide them with appropriate instruments of protection. For Christian dignity, as also human dignity, is the source and root of fundamental rights and duties with regard to the common call to holiness and to the spread of the Kingdom of God: these are the rights and duties of Christians. This is the juridical situation common to all the faithful, whatever their particular function in the Church.[2]

On this basis, the *Coetus* went on to outline a project which would include a basic definition of a *Christifidelis*, a description of his basic rights and duties, and procedures, both judicial and administrative, to safeguard them.[3] This can serve as a useful outline of the present review of the status of the faithful in the new Code.

1. THE DEFINITION OF A CHRISTIAN BELIEVER

Book II of SCIC is entitled *De Populo Dei* and begins with a section 'On the Christian Faithful'. This contains two fundamental canons on the common status of believers and on the distinctions among them. Canon 201 reads:

> The Christian faithful are those who, because by baptism incorporated into Christ, are established in the people of God and who for this reason, sharing in their own way in the priestly, prophetical, and kingly rôle of Christ, are called, according to the proper juridical condition of each, to carry out the mission which God gave the Church to fulfil in the world.

This canon draws upon the typological definition of a layman in LG § 31. The only significant departure from the conciliar text is the introduction of the phrase, 'according to the proper juridical condition of each', which rather nervously anticipates the distinctions of canon 202. There it is stated that 'by divine institution there are in the Church sacred ministers, who in the law are called clerics, and other faithful, who are called laypeople'; paragraph 2 then states that there are also religious who can belong to either state. As it stands now, Book II goes on to devote sixty-six canons to clerics, twenty-one of which concern their duties and rights, and eight canons to the duties and rights of the laity. The section on common duties and rights has apparently been deferred to the LEF. To determine what this material may look like, one must fall back upon the most recent reports of the pertinent *Coetus*.

The *Coetus De Populo Dei* elaborated two other basic canons, each of which has a parallel in the work of the *Coetus* on the LEF. The first of these (c. 17 in SDPD), as most recently revised, reads:

> The obligations and rights which are set down in the following canons are proper to all the faithful insofar as they are in ecclesiastical communion, whether they be clerics or laypeople, and without discrimination among them on the basis of sex, race, nation, or social condition.[4]

The next proposed canon asserts the basic equality of all believers:

> Although in the Church of Christ there are different offices and rôles, all must acknowledge the true equality which obtains among them by virtue of their common baptism and they must respect the fraternity by which they are for this reason linked to one another.[5]

The parallel text in LEF reads:

> Among all Christian believers, by virtue of their rebirth in Christ, there obtains a true equality with regard to their dignity and to the activity by which all, each indeed according to his own condition and proper rôle, work together to build up the Body of Christ.[6]

These canons are intended to reflect the statements of LG § 32. Clearly, it is valuable to have the Council's insistence on equality and repudiation of discrimination in the Church's new lawbook. Wherever placed, these statements will provide a norm by which the new Code itself must be judged, not to mention any other general or particular legislation. For that reason, one must regret certain changes which have been made in the Council's text.

The most important of these affects the equality of common activity. The Council spoke of a true equality 'with regard to the dignity and activity common to all the faithful with respect to the building up of the Body of Christ' (LG § 32). Reference to a 'common activity' has quite disappeared from the SDPD text and in LEF it is altered to 'an activity by which all, each indeed according to his own condition and proper rôle, work together to build up the Body of Christ'. The activity is no longer called 'common' and now, in the midst of a judgment about equality, there is an assertion of distinctions of condition and rôle. These changes might not be considered major did we not know that they were introduced into both texts because certain members of the *Coetus* felt that the conciliar text had been misinterpreted 'with very dangerous consequences for the life of the Church, for there really is no equality of action'.[7] The changes, therefore, are not at all innocent.

All the texts of the new Code will, it seems, speak of 'obligations and rights' rather than of 'rights and obligations'. The preference for that order is explained in the report of the *Coetus De Populo Dei*, several of whose consultors along with the Relator affirmed that 'rights flow from duties'.[8] This statement reflects a clear choice among competing theories of rights in the Church and helps to explain why there are so many references in these and in other canons to qualifications by virtue of juridical status. The presence of these qualifications in statements of basic rights somewhat restricts the affirmation of a true and common equality. The theory of rights that appears to lie behind them is difficult to reconcile with the many statements of recent popes, of the Council, and even of several canons in the new Code, which make rights and duties flow, without specified priority, from a common source, variously described as God, Christ, the Holy Spirit, baptism, confirmation, created dignity, etc.

The matter is of particular importance with regard to the status of women in the Church. While discrimination on the basis of sex has been eliminated from the basic canons *De personis*,[9] it continues to appear, for no apparent reason, when the official ministries of lector and acolyte are restricted to men (SCIC 275:1) and when only lay*men* can serve as ecclesiastical judges (SCIC 1373:2).[10]

2. THE BASIC RIGHTS COMMON TO ALL THE FAITHFUL

So far as we can judge now, the LEF will include the fundamental and common statute on the obligations and rights of all the faithful which the *Coetus* on the Laity had hoped for as a way of overcoming the 'stratified ecclesiology' of the old Code.[11] The new Code will enumerate the following common duties: keeping and professing the faith, maintaining communion with the Church, acquiring a knowledge of Christian doctrine, spreading the gospel, pursuing a holy life and helping the Church to grow, making their views known to their pastors, meeting the needs of the Church, respecting the common good and the rights of others, promoting ecumenism, working for social justice, and, for parents, seeing to the Christian education of their children. The rights common to all the faithful will be those of receiving the spiritual goods of the Church, participating in the liturgy, worshipping in their own rite and following their own form of spirituality, founding and directing their own associations, making their needs, desires, and opinions known, by their own initiative promoting and sustaining apostolic activities, receiving a Christian education and seeing that their children receive one, enjoying freedom of inquiry, freely choosing a state in life, having their good name respected, freedom from canonical penalty except according to the law, vindicating and defending their rights in a competent Church forum, and being judged with equity and according to the law.

This is a substantial list of rights, including, I believe, all but one of the rights affirmed in the Council. While, as will be observed shortly, one may have reservations about particular canons and about the nervousness with which many rights are stated, it would be wrong to ignore what a great advance this represents in comparison with the old Code. This is particularly true of the laity who, of course, enjoy all the rights and are bound by all the duties just listed. They thus have a right to take part in evangelisation and in the apostolate (LEF 11, 16); they have their own part in the saving mission of the Church (LEF 28); they share in the priestly, prophetical, and kingly rôle of Christ (LEF 56:2). In various canons these rights are said to be grounded in baptism and confirmation or to be a deputation from God. Correspondingly, clerics are reminded to acknowledge and promote their rôle in the Church and in the world (LEF 26; SCIC 248:2; 361).[12]

The proposed texts also go beyond the old Code in stating the ability of the laity to be involved more 'officially' in the Church's work. Where the old Code had said that 'only clerics can receive the power of orders or of ecclesiastical jurisdiction' (SCIC 118), the new Code will say, 'only clerics can obtain offices for whose exercise is required the power of orders or a power of ecclesiastical governance that rests upon the power of orders' (SCIC 244). The laity are said to be qualified (*habiles*) to be entrusted with ecclesiastical offices and tasks and to serve as experts and advisers (SCIC 273). They have a right to pursue higher studies in the sacred sciences in ecclesiastical universities and elsewhere, and they can receive the *missio docendi* (SCIC 274:2-3). In the absence of ordained ministers, acolytes and lectors, they can supply certain of their offices, namely the ministry of the Word, presiding over liturgical prayers, conferring baptism and distributing communion (SCIC 275:3). When priests are scarce, they can also be entrusted with a share in the exercise of pastoral care (SCIC 455:2).

In these canons, the conciliar statements on official relationships between laity and hierarchy are reflected and respected (see LG 33, 35; AA 17, 24). The remarkable developments of lay ministries which have taken place since the Council, while not adequately represented in the proposed texts, are also not (or at least not yet) seriously challenged by them, even if the new ministries are presented only as exceptions permitted because of the scarcity of official or ordained ministers. However, the *Coetus* on the LEF has referred to the Sacred Congregation for the Doctrine of the Faith two questions whose determination will be crucial for the future: (1) whether or not legislative or judicial authority can be entrusted to laypeople, and (2) what are 'the ecclesiastical tasks to be exercised for a spiritual purpose' which, according to LG § 33 (repeated in LEF 56:3), can be entrusted to laypeople.[13]

Notably lacking in the proposed texts is any reference to one of the most important assertions of a right and duty in the texts of Vatican II. I refer to *Apostolicam actuositatem* § 3:

> From the reception of these charisms, even the most ordinary ones, there arise for each of the faithful the right and duty to exercise them in the Church and in the world for the good of men and the upbuilding of the Church, in the freedom of the Holy Spirit "who breathes where he will", and at the same time in communion with their brethren in Christ, especially with their pastors, whose rôle it is to judge the authenticity and orderly exercise of the gifts, not indeed in order to extinguish the Spirit but to test all things and to keep what is good.

Nowhere is this text even alluded to in the present canons; in fact, there is only one passing reference to charisms.[14]

This omission did not escape notice, for there was a discussion in the *Coetus* on the LEF as to whether to accept a proposal to add a new canon 'which in a general and programmatic way would acknowledge for the faithful the free and orderly exercise of personal charisms and at the same time would affirm their obligation to subordinate this exercise to the demands of charity'. After the Relator replied that this was a good text, but not 'juridical', a discussion ensued on whether what the canon intends is not already taken care of in a number of particular canons. It was finally decided to make some mention of charisms, but to do so in the theological introduction to the LEF and not in a separate canon.[15]

While one may be happy that some mention of charisms will be made somewhere, one may regret that it will not receive particular mention in a distinct canon. It certainly deserves notice as much as many another item honoured with its own canon; perhaps it deserves it even more, since it represents a justification of ministries not reflected elsewhere in these texts. Other texts refer ministries and activities to Christ and to the sacraments, but the perspectives of AA § 3 and of LG 12[16] are absent. The new texts thus miss an opportunity to integrate into their ecclesiology the work of the Spirit as a permanent source of the variety of services and ministries in the Church.[17]

There is another reason for regretting the neglect of AA § 3. This conciliar text speaks of the charisms being exercised at once in the freedom of the Spirit and in communion with others, particularly pastors. While the latter have the rôle of judging the authenticity of the gifts, this is to be donè under the apostolic injunction not to quench the Spirit. These criteria are poorly represented in a text such as LEF 24:

> § 1. In exercising their rights, both individuals and those joined in associations must take account of the common good of the Church as well as of the rights of others and of their own duties towards them.
>
> § 2. It belongs to ecclesiastical authority in view of the common good to direct the exercise of the rights which are proper to Christians and to restrict them by invalidating or disqualifying laws.[18]

The spiritual confidence of the Council's statement is absent from this canon, whose language and emphasis reflect much more an ecclesiology of hierarchical direction and restriction than one of freedom and communion. Instead of expecting benefits from the gifts of the Spirit, there is a fear of the common good's being infringed and an expectation of a need for invalidating and disqualifying laws; and nowhere is the apostle's warning recalled.[19]

To discuss all the canons in which the rights of the faithful are stated and to determine to what degree they are respected in the provisions of SCIC would far exceed the permitted bounds of this essay. It appears that a mixed judgment would have to be made: many canons faithfully echo Vatican II, others introduce needless restrictions; many ecclesial rights are rather well provided for, others are poorly reflected. For the future, it will be important to establish the hermeneutical principles that the new Code is to be interpreted in the light of the Council and not vice-versa, and that the interpretation and implementation of the Code must follow the statements of basic rights and not vice-versa.

Finally, it should certainly be noted that the new texts also affirm the Church's duty to acknowledge, respect, and defend the basic rights of all human beings whether members of the Church or not. This principle is clearly stated in LEF 3, although similar canons have been dropped from SDPD.[20] LEF 51:1 speaks of the inalienable rights which a temporal order must preserve, and LEF 57:2 vindicates the right of the Church to pass judgment on societies in so far as 'fundamental rights and the salvation of souls require it'.[21] Unfortunately, the Church's rôle in temporal societies is evacuated of much of its prophetic character in the latest revision of LEF 51:2.[22]

3. PROCEDURES FOR THE PROTECTION OF RIGHTS

The Guiding Principles for the revision of the Code envisaged a procedure which would be applicable to both superiors and subjects 'so that any suspicion of arbitrariness might quite vanish in ecclesiastical administration'.[23] The *Coetus* on the Laity endorsed this principle and declared it to include certain rights, 'namely, that the parties in a case always be heard and enjoy sponsorship, the right to know the name of an accuser whenever a procedure is brought against a believer because of a denunciation, and the right to know the reasons on which a decision or judgment against him rests'.[24]

In the proposed texts, LEF 22 provides that the faithful have the right to vindicate and defend their rights in a competent ecclesiastical forum and, should they be called to judgment, that they be judged according to the law and with equity.[25] If the *Coetus De Populo Dei* has its way, to this canon will be added a provision for a right of recourse against an administrative action by which a person believes himself to have been injured.[26] SDPD 36 had stated five rights which the faithful have with regard to procedures brought against them, but these have been dropped or transferred for discussion, on the grounds that they are sufficiently provided for in the canons *De processibus*.[27] At least one of these rights, however, that of knowing the name of one's accuser is not retained in that section.

The clear statement of SDPD 34, that the faithful have the right of recourse against an authority which exceeds its competence or uses its power for a purpose not intended by the law, is not well represented in the proposed Code. SCIC 1352:2 states that 'controversies arising because of an action of an administrative authority can only be brought to a superior or to an administrative tribunal'. But the canons *De procedura administrativa* have most recently been revised to make facultative the establishment of administrative tribunals whether by Episcopal Conference or by dioceses.[28] The right of recourse mentioned in SCIC 1702 and 1704, therefore, may prove to be no right at all, if such a tribunal is not set up. An initial examination thus suggests that the new Code does not adequately provide for the defence of the rights which it is itself to assert.

CONCLUSION

By comparison with the old Code, the proposed texts represent an important ecclesiological advance, particularly with regard to the status of the laity, who no longer appear merely as the passive recipients of the clergy's ministrations. By comparison to Vatican II, the proposed texts are generally faithful in mentioning the rights noted in the Council documents; but a certain nervousness is also evident, especially in the subordination of rights to duties and in the many qualifications introduced. The common status of all believers is barely mentioned before distinctions are introduced, almost as if equality were considered to mean identity and to exclude diversity and differentiation. Furthermore, changes are also introduced in the conciliar texts on the basis of a rather negative evaluation of post-conciliar developments. It will, therefore, be of some importance to establish the traditional criterion that laws are to be interpreted as written and not simply on the basis of the legislator's or drafter's supposed motives. Finally, as briefly mentioned earlier, the new Code should not be assigned doctrinal value independent of, much less superior to, that of the teachings of Vatican II, which remains the more adequate and more authoritative statement of the Church's self-understanding.

Notes

1. *Communicationes* 1 (1969) 82-83.
2. *Comm.* 2 (1970) 91; see also p. 93.
3. *Ibid.* pp. 92-93.
4. *Comm.* 12 (1980) 78; LEF 7 reads: 'By baptism a man is incorporated into the Church of Christ and therein constituted a person, with the duties and rights which, in accordance with their condition, are proper to Christians in so far as they are in ecclesiastical communion and unless some legitimate sanction poses an obstacle' (*ibid.* p. 33).
5. *Ibid.* p. 79.
6. *Ibid.* p. 36.
7. *Ibid.* pp. 35-36; see also p. 79. These reports confirm the remarks of G. Thils 'La Révision du droit canonique et les problèmes ecclésiologiques qu'elle rencontre' *Rev. theol. Louv.* 9 (1978) 333-338.
8. *Comm.* 12 (1980) 78.
9. *Ibid.* pp. 65-77.
10. See also SCIC 1692, where only 'fit priests' can serve as members of administrative tribunals; SCIC 977, of course, states that only men can validly receive the sacrament of order.
11. *Comm.* 2 (1970) 94-96.
12. The special responsibilities of the laity for the secular order are mentioned in SCIC 270:2 and their freedom in secular affairs guaranteed in SCIC 272.
13. *Comm.* 9 (1977) 288, 293; see H. Socha 'Der Dienst der Pastoralreferenten und die eine geistliche Vollmacht' *Arch. kath. Kirchenrecht* 147 (1978) 377-405. Meanwhile, the laity have only a consultative rôle in diocesan synods, pastoral councils, and particular councils. Deep suspicion of lay involvement in legislative process is reflected in *Comm.* 9 (1977) 285-288.
14. LEF 26; see *Comm.* 12 (1980) 46, and compare the text to LG § 30.

15. *Comm.* 12 (1980) 43-44; very little information is available on the nature or content of the theological preface.

16. LG § 12 speaks of the 'special graces' by which the Spirit makes the faithful 'fit and ready to undertake various works and offices for the renewal and further upbuilding of the Church'.

17. See P. Lombardia 'Relevancia de los carismos personales en el ordenamiento canonico' *Ius Can.* 9 (1969) 101-119; G. Thils 'La Révision . . .' pp. 338-341.

18. *Comm.* 12 (1980) 43.

19. LEF 55:2 establishes that the office of governing must direct the exercise of the other two chief tasks of the Church. While this can be given a good sense, it needs to be balanced by clear statements of the objective limits which the character of the Church's preaching and sacramental rôles imply.

20. *Comm.* 12 (1980) 32, 90-91.

21. *Ibid.* pp. 98-100, 106-107.

22. *Ibid.* p. 100.

23. *Comm.* 1 (1969) 83.

24. *Comm.* 2 (1970) 93.

25. *Comm.* 12 (1980) 42.

26. *Ibid.* p. 88.

27. *Ibid.* pp. 89-90.

28. See *Schema Codias Iuris Canonici*, canon 1689 § 1.

Thomas Green

The Use of Vatican II Texts in the Draft *De Populo Dei*

1. INTRODUCTION: STRUCTURE OF THE DRAFT

AN ESPECIALLY significant project of the Code Commission has been the draft *De Populo Dei*, forwarded for evaluation to the world episcopate and other consultative bodies in early 1978. Along with the *Lex Fundamentalis*, this draft is of the greatest theoretical-practical importance since it clarifies the status of believers and specifies how the Church is structured at various levels. A brief overview of its structure can illustrate its comprehensive scope and relevance to the Church's legal-pastoral life.[1]

Part I of the draft (1-80) deals with the status of 'persons in general'. An initial norm on membership is followed by provisions on the canonical status of physical persons (2-15) and on the fundamental duties and rights of believers (16-38). A detailed treatment of associations of the faithful (39-69) then precedes a brief discussion of juridical (formerly moral) persons (70-80).

Part II of the draft (81-533) considers various issues under the general rubric 'persons in particular'. It is subdivided into four main sections: sacred ministers or clerics (81-154), the Church's hierarchical constitution (155-397), religious (398-522)[2] and the obligations and rights of the laity and lay associations (523-533).

Some further clarifications of the first two categories seem appropriate. The section on clerics considers their formation (82-119), incardination (120-127) and basic obligations and rights (128-149); it also treats of the loss of the clerical state (150-154).

The section on the Church's hierarchical constitution treats of the organisation of the people of God at various levels. Title 1 deals with the exercise of supreme authority in the Church (155-184); it considers the Roman Pontiff and the College of Bishops (155-156), the Synod of Bishops (157-163), the College of Cardinals (164-175), the Roman Curia (176) and papal legates (177-184). Title 2 specifies norms for the exercise of authority within the particular churches and in the groupings of such churches (185-397). An initial chapter considers different dimensions of supra-diocesan government: the union of the particular churches in regions and provinces (185-188), regional and provincial councils (189-198), episcopal conferences (199-210) and metropolitans/primates (211-216). The second chapter concerns various issues of diocesan, parish and deanery organisations (217-297). After clarifying the basic elements of diocesan organisation (217-224), the draft discusses bishops in general

(225-232), diocesan bishops (233-260) and coadjutors and auxiliaries (261-269). Subsequently it considers various diocesan institutes mentioned in the Code: the diocesan synod (270-280), the Diocesan Curia (281-308), the Chapter of Canons (317-325) and the impeded or vacant see (330-348). The draft also regulates newer conciliar-inspired entities such as the Council (senate) of Priests (309-315), the College of Consultors (316) and the pastoral council (326-329). The final issues dealt with are parishes and pastors (349-376), parochial vicars (377-384) and deans (385-389).

2. EVALUATION OF THE DRAFT

Since the draft was issued only relatively recently, there are few analyses available in professional journals.[3] The author of this article has prepared some reflections on the draft in light of the evaluations of professional canonical societies in Australia, the British Isles, Canada and the United States. These hitherto unpublished reflections[4] will be employed in commenting on the draft's use of conciliar sources.

A responsible assessment of the draft presupposes certain criteria of judgment. Obviously a fundamental point of reference must be the draft's fidelity to Vatican II, particularly *Lumen gentium* and *Christus Dominus*, its key conciliar sources. Particularly significant post-conciliar implementing documents such as *Ecclesiae sanctae*[5] should also be considered. Furthermore, a key standard against which the draft must be measured are the principles for the revision of the Code approved by the 1967 Synod of Bishops.[6] Finally, the draft must be examined in terms of contemporary pastoral needs and experience since a judgment that it will be good law depends largely on whether it will foster the responsible involvement of all believers in carrying out the Church's mission.

Limitations of space require our focusing attention on the most significant criterion in analysing the draft, i.e., its fidelity to the principal orientations of Vatican II. Such limitations as well as the comprehensiveness of the draft also make it necessary to limit the following considerations to selected issues of canonical reform. An examination of these issues, however, should help clarify how carefully the draft utilises conciliar sources. In this connection the author employs certain principles of institutional reform first articulated by the Austrian pastoral theologian Ferdinand Klostermann[7] and later refined in light of other theological-canonical insights.[8]

At the outset one should mention certain problems in analysing the draft. First of all, the latest version of the *Lex Fundamentalis* is unavailable; yet the draft refers to it regarding several significant issues such as the relationship between the pope and the College of Bishops and the basic obligations and rights of believers.[9] No fully satisfactory examination of the draft can be made without access to the *Lex*, which also deals with fundamental theological-canonical issues affecting the Church's organisation for mission. Secondly, unlike the *Lex*, no explanatory *relatio* accompanies the draft; and hence it is difficult at times to discern the precise intent of its authors. The problem may be complicated by the fact that the draft is not the product of a single Code Commission *coetus* but rather of four such sub-committees.[10] Furthermore, except for occasional references in the *Praenotanda* and some notations in the section on clerical formation, the draft normally fails to indicate its theological-canonical sources.

3. THE USE OF CONCILIAR SOURCES IN THE DRAFT

In fairness it should be observed that the draft is reasonably faithful to its conciliar sources in numerous areas; and examples of such fidelity will be duly cited.

Nevertheless, the main burden of the following reflections will be to clarify some noteworthy problems in the draft's handling of conciliar sources. If the new law is to embody the best insights of our theological-canonical tradition, these concerns must be addressed seriously. The general rubric 'inadequate use of conciliar sources' can mean different things. At times the draft directly contradicts conciliar sources. Occasionally sources are selectively cited or are taken out of their proper context. More often the problem is not precisely that a given conciliar text has been used incorrectly but rather that an orientation indicated by various conciliar sources has not been taken seriously in the reform of canonical institutes. As noted earlier the draft will be examined in light of certain principles of institutional reform. A brief description of each principle will be followed by specific examples of its implications for the draft's use of sources. At times the principles tend to overlap since they are somewhat artificial efforts to deal with complex conciliar data and their relevance to contemporary institutional reform.[11] Furthermore there is no particular reason for the order in which the various principles are treated.

4. PNEUMATIC-CHARISMATIC PRINCIPLE[12]

Conciliar documents such as *Gaudium et spes* and *Dignitatis humanae* highlight the dignity of the human person. Furthermore, principles 6 and 7 for the revision of the Code stress the need to remedy legal deficiencies regarding the protection of personal rights. Another significant conciliar datum is the enhanced sensitivity to the ecclesial rôle of the Spirit, who endows all believers with charismatic gifts and not simply those in positions of authority.

Accordingly, the pneumatic-charismatic principle means that ecclesial structures should foster the discernment and exercise of the manifold gifts of the Spirit. A significant legal concern is articulating the basic rights and obligations of believers and creating appropriate structures to protect free exercise of those rights within the community.

The draft is to be praised for its effort to specify the basic rights and obligations of believers (16-38). This represents a significant change from the Code with its explicit reference to the rights of believers only in canon 87 on the implications of baptism/Church membership and canon 682 on the reception of various spiritual goods necessary for salvation. Furthermore norms 39-69 strive to clarify the implications of the fundamental right of association of all believers (31, 1) and specifically of clerics (137). However, like the *Lex*, the draft raises profound problems in its discussion of the basic rights/obligations of believers. It tends to over-emphasise obligations rather than rights. The expression of rights is overly qualified so that the limitations of rights seem essential to the notion of the right itself and not related to its responsible exercise. The significance of baptism and confirmation for fundamental Christian rights is hardly as strongly emphasised as in *Lumen gentium* or *Apostolicam actuositatem*. The laity at times seem to be viewed more as subjects of the hierarchy than as mature Christians with a sacramentally-grounded dignity and right to share in the Church's mission. Finally the draft does not take seriously enough the legal significance of charisms, which partly ground the right of the laity to share in the Church's mission in their own distinctive fashion and not simply in a way derivative of the apostolate of the hierarchy.[13]

The contemporary concern about the ecclesial rôle of women might profitably be dealt with here although this issue should be seen within the broader framework of the status of the non-ordained to be treated next. Certain norms in the draft enhance the legal status of women. Norm 17, 1 prohibits sex discrimination regarding basic Christian rights and obligations. Norm 193 requires the presence of major superiors of women's communities at plenary and provincial councils while providing for the facultative presence of other women. Norm 273 requires that superiors of women's communities be present at diocesan synods; it likewise provides for the facultative presence of other women, e.g., as representatives of the diocesan pastoral council. Unfortunately other norms are rather sexist in character. Norms 9 and 14 on domicile and rite are inadequately sensitive to the conciliar stress on conjugal equality. No provision is made for women religious at the Synod of Bishops unlike members of clerical institutes. Norm 529, 1 unfortunately prohibits women from being installed in lay ministries which they may exercise in virtue of 529, 2-3.

5. PRINCIPLE OF FUNDAMENTAL CHRISTIAN EQUALITY AND CO-RESPONSIBILITY[14]

A key conciliar insight was the clarification of the fundamental equality of all believers regarding certain primordial ecclesial realities: baptism, destiny, Lord and mission. (*Lumen gentium* §§ 9 and 32.) That this equality precedes structural differentiations rooted in orders is evident in part from the situation of chapter 2 of *Lumen gentium* on the people of God prior to chapter 3 on the hierarchy.

This means that a reformed legal order should avoid paternalistic patterns of governance reflecting the stratified ecclesiology of the Code. On the contrary the new law should foster both functional diversity and a profound spirit of communion in the realisation of the Church's mission. If the new law is really to be a law of the people of God, it must direct and promote the life of the whole ecclesial community and not simply specify how ordained ministers share in the Church's mission. In fact this may be the principal issue underlying the critiques of various drafts of the revised law over the past decade and a half.

It would be unfair to say that the draft takes no cognisance of such concerns. Its effort to clarify the basic rights and obligations of believers and its provisions for lay involvement in various conciliar processes at the national, provincial and diocesan church levels bear witness to the draft's attempt to respond to conciliar expectations. However, like the *Lex*, a major problem is the draft's tendency to view the realisation of the Church's mission from an overly hierarchical and minimally communitarian perspective. Although both the *Lex* and the draft improve the Code, their fundamental approach needs to be significantly reworked if they are to do justice to chapter 2 of *Lumen gentium* and paragraphs 33-36 of chapter 4.

Some examples will indicate the overly hierarchical horizons of the draft. It tends to view formation for ministry almost exclusively in clerical and more specifically in priestly terms (82-119). Yet the conciliar-inspired emergence of a plurality of ministries suggests that ministerial formation should be viewed in a more broadly ecclesial fashion. There should be greater interaction between those preparing for ordained ministry and those committing themselves to various forms of non-ordained ministry in the Church.

The norms on the Synod of Bishops (157-163) make it clear that it is almost exclusively an episcopal body and certainly an entirely clerical one. While this reflects the 1965 *Motu proprio 'Apostolica sollicitudo'*,[15] fidelity to Vatican II may suggest the wisdom of its being *de iure* a gathering of the whole Church and not simply of bishops. In fact this would be consistent with the pattern of so-called 'mixed councils' at all other levels of the Church involving representatives of the whole people of God with a consultative voice.

Norm 228 on the selection of bishops improves the Code *vis-à-vis* episcopal involvement in the process; yet it still seems notably lacking regarding the other members of the particular church. This is true both in regard to ascertaining diocesan needs and clarifying the requisite qualities of potential bishops. Such involvement of an informed cross-section of the people of God seems a logical corollary of the draft's affirmation of the basic Christian right to participate in the pursuit of the Church's mission and to express one's opinion on issues affecting the Church's well-being (27-28/*Lumen gentium* § 37).

The draft's provisions for diocesan pastoral councils seem notably impoverished in contrast to its conciliar and post-conciliar sources (326-329). *Christus Dominus* § 27 spoke of this institute as highly desirable (*valde optandum*), and this was also true in *Ecclesiae sanctae* I, 16 and the Directory on the Pastoral Ministry of Bishops[16] § 204. However norm 326 speaks of their establishment only to the extent that pastoral solicitude suggests it (*quatenus pastoralis sollicitudo id suadeat*); and norm 248, 1 calls for bishops to establish such bodies only to the extent that circumstances permit it (*quantum adiuncta id sinant*). Undeniably circumstances differ throughout the Church so that in some places the specific form of the pastoral council indicated in the official documents may not be possible. However, a basic legal principle to be stressed is the bishop's responsibility to introduce suitable consultative organs according to diocesan needs and resources.

The section on parishes has some positive features, e.g., provisions for non-clerics in leadership positions in the absence of clerics (349, 3). However, practically speaking this part of the draft considers pastors almost exclusively with hardly any attention given to other members of the parish community. There is no reference to parish councils or comparable consultative bodies in view of fostering collaboration in realising the Church's mission. (*Pastoral Directory* 179; *Apostolicam actuositatem* 10 and 26.) Unlike norms 249-250 which speak of the bishop's responsibility to foster lay initiatives, this part of the draft specifies nothing comparable for pastors. It reflects *Christus Dominus* § 30, 1-2 on the pastor's cultic and magisterial responsibilities; yet it hardly corresponds to 30, 3 on his pastoral leadership rôle.

6. PRINCIPLE OF COLLEGIALITY[17]

A genuinely sound Church order must reflect the vital interrelationship between the pope and the College of Bishops in the governance of the universal Church. Structuring this complex relationship so as to do justice to the uniqueness of the papal office and to respect the vital rôle of the college in the life of the Church has never been easy. However, it is a fundamental issue in post-conciliar legal reform and therefore it furnishes an important perspective from which to judge the adequacy of the draft.

As noted earlier this part of the draft is difficult to evaluate without access to the *Lex*, which apparently treats of certain key issues related to collegiality, e.g., ecumenical council. Nevertheless certain issues can be commented on briefly.

First of all the section on supreme Church authority (155-184) reflects reasonably well those aspects of Vatican II dealing with the pope; however, it systematically deletes references to the solicitude of the bishops for the universal Church. The initial norms 155-156 view the Synod of Bishops, the College of Cardinals and the Roman Curia in the same way in terms of their service to the Roman Pontiff in the personal exercise of his primatial office. This hardly does justice to all the relevant ecclesiological values, among which is that of the Synod as representative of the College of Bishops and a symbol of concern for the universal Church (*Christus Dominus* § 5 and *Apostolica sollicitudo* § 1). Furthermore, the Synod's potential for deliberative competence is expressed somewhat more negatively in the draft (158) than in *Apostolica sollicitudo* II. It may be premature to seek a more meaningful deliberative rôle for the Synod; yet the draft should not preclude its functioning in a more genuinely collaborative rôle with the pope in the future.

Another related issue is the relationship of the College of Bishops to the Roman Curia. Since the draft contains no norms on specific curial dicasteries, it is hard to assess this institute properly. Yet one particularly unsatisfactory feature of the draft is its referring to the Curia's service of the pope alone in dealing with issues affecting the universal Church (156, 3 and 176). This neglects the conciliar stress on the Curia's being seen in service to the College of Bishops as well (*Christus Dominus* § 9).

Technically collegiality refers to the relationship between the pope and the College of Bishops; however, by way of analogy one might briefly consider the relationship of the bishop and the Council of Priests under this general rubric. The draft reasonably faithfully reflects the present law on this institute (309-315); it largely restates *Ecclesiae sanctae* I, 15 and selected excerpts from the 1970 circular letter of the Congregation for the Clergy.[18] However, certain aspects of the draft pose problems because they seem to preclude the possibility of significant developments in the relationship between bishop and presbyters envisioned in *Presbyterorum ordinis* § 7. The draft (314, 2) significantly limits the potential deliberative competence of such councils; this corresponds to present law but it contradicts the openness of number 9 of the circular letter on this point. Norm 315, 3 provides for possible episcopal dissolution of the Council if it does not fulfill or if it seriously abuses its diocesan responsibilities. Unfortunately there seems to be no provision for recourse to the metropolitan or some other supra-diocesan institute to preclude possibly arbitrary episcopal discretion. Finally norm 315, 2 on the cessation of the council *sede vacante* reflects the present legal situation. However, it might well remain in existence in view of symbolising the continuity of the presbyterate in such a situation.

7. PRINCIPLE OF SUBSIDIARITY[19]

Particularly since Vatican II there has been a renewed awareness of the need to respect diverse legal-cultural traditions in the particular churches. The fostering of an ecclesial unity that is not equivalent to uniformity is necessary if the different gifts of the Spirit are to flourish (*Lumen gentium* § 23; *Orientalium ecclesiarum* § 2). After centuries of increasingly centralised government, a significant post-conciliar task is shaping a genuine canonical pluralism comparable to the theological, liturgical and ascetical diversity explicitly welcomed by Vatican II. That this is a delicate enterprise is clear from the formulation of principle 5 for the revision of the Code. It stresses that there must be a fundamental unity in basic principles of Church order and in its fundamental institutions; yet it emphasises the importance of greater latitude for creative initiatives in the particular churches. However, it seems more open to such initiatives in the Eastern churches than in the Latin church.

The basic issue here is the relative decisional pre-eminence of the Holy See, the episcopal conference and the individual bishop in various issues. To what extent do certain ecclesial issues have to be resolved at the level of the Holy See if the unity or well-being of all the churches is to be fostered? Furthermore, to what extent do certain ecclesial issues have to be resolved by the episcopal conference rather than by the diocesan bishop if the unity or well-being of the Church in a given area is to be enhanced? As might be expected, this has been a major concern in the examination of various Code Commission drafts and not simply the draft *De Populo Dei*.

Frankly the draft is to be commended for its increased recognition of the rôle of the episcopal conference, whose treatment largely corresponds to the conciliar sources (199-210). Approximately twenty-seven norms reserve decisions in various areas to the conference, e.g., training of clergy, establishment of particular churches on other than territorial grounds, the ordering of liturgical life, the appointment of pastors for limited terms of office, etc.

However, critics of the draft raise significant questions about whether the principle of subsidiarity (infra-universal decisional autonomy) might be implemented still more fully without impairing Church unity. The size and diversity of the Latin church(es) and the uniqueness of individual churches within the *communio* need to be taken more seriously. Norms that may be appropriate in Western Europe and North America may be quite inappropriate in Africa, Asia or Latin America. For example, questions have been raised about the realism of the detailed norms on the Diocesan Curia (281-308) especially in so-called Third World nations. More significant an issue is the matter of fashioning new ministerial forms responding to the shifting patterns of post-conciliar ecclesial ministry. This has implications for such matters as the creation of new ministries, the changing rôle of women in the Church and the restructuring of parish leadership rôles among others. There should be significant latitude for the discretion of the episcopal conference or of the individual bishop in response to diverse pastoral exigencies. Needless to say, this presupposes consultation with the Holy See and other episcopal conferences lest ecclesial unity be significantly jeopardised.

A related concern is ministerial formation and education. The provisions for greater latitude for infra-universal legislators are welcome. However, the draft's laudable intention to provide for socio-cultural diversity is somewhat compromised by overly detailed norms on ministerial formation (82-119). The draft should be streamlined to provide general principles on such formation to be specified largely through appropriate episcopal conference directories (*Christus Dominus* § 44).

Another aspect problematic of the principle of subsidiarity is the relationship between the episcopal conference and the individual bishop. While the increased competence of the conference may generally be welcome, there may be the danger of creating an intermediary decisional power as inadequately sensitive to diverse ecclesial circumstances as an overly centralised Code. Hence there is a crucial need to reassert the legitimate pastoral discretion of the individual bishop in shaping the mission of the particular church in consultation with appropriate corporate bodies and individuals (*Christus Dominus* § 8). That discretion should be limited only if absolutely necessary to foster the unity or well-being of the whole Church or the Church in a given area.

Questions can be posed about the adequacy of the draft's provisions for episcopal discretion in several areas. This seems particularly true regarding the bishop's power to dispense from universal law (246) where the draft is more restrictive than *Christus Dominus* 8b or the 1966 *Motu proprio De episcoporum muneribus*.[20] American critics of the draft have questioned its continued reservation of dispensations from celibacy to the Holy See. The bishop/religious superior who has guided the priest during his years of ministerial formation and service seems generally in the best position to judge the adequacy of his reasons for resignation from the active ministry in light of all the relevant values to be considered. Finally, and more significantly, there seems to be an unwarranted limitation of the bishop's ability to delegate his legislative authority in contrast to his freedom to do so in administrative and judicial areas (244, 3 and norm 102, 1 of the general norms draft). The bishop should be able to delegate such legislative power to a corporate body such as a diocesan synod or conciliar bodies such as the Council of Priests or the diocesan pastoral council should it be appropriate to do so.

8. CONCLUSION

These brief reflections have attempted to clarify certain aspects of the much broader question of the draft's use of conciliar sources. They have indicated some noteworthy problems even though the draft must be credited with some genuine accomplishments in translating conciliar principles into workable norms of action. The seriousness of the problems in the draft and the difficulties identified in other drafts make it imperative that these texts be seriously reworked by the appropriate Code Commission sub-committees and resubmitted to the bishops and other consultative organs before promulgation of the new Code. Unfortunately at the time of writing of this article, such further consultation seems highly unlikely although not impossible.

Perhaps still more important in the long run is the task of fashioning models of legislative renewal at all levels of the Church. This is indispensable if we are to take seriously the conciliar vision of a pilgrim community constantly called to reform as it moves through history and strives to read the signs of the times (*Lumen gentium* § 9; *Gaudium et spes* § 4). The ongoing *aggiornamento* of canonical institutes in response to changing theological-pastoral exigencies is crucial if Church law is to be a vital force in serving the Church's salvific mission.

Notes

1. The numbers in parentheses refer to particular 'norms' in the draft. The term 'norms' designates the legal provisions of the draft as opposed to the 'canons' of the Code.

2. The provisions on religious were not actually included in the draft *De Populo Dei* since they had been forwarded separately for evaluation purposes in early 1977.

3. For an examination of the norms on physical persons see H. Muller 'Ius condendum de personis in genere' *Periodica* 68 (1979) 119-137. For some observations on the draft among other issues see G. Sheehy 'Reflections on the Current State of Law in the Church' *Studia Canonica* 12 (1978) 199-210.

4. The proposed article is entitled 'Critical Reflections on the Schema on the People of God'; it is expected to appear in the second issue of *Studia Canonica* 14 (1980). For a briefer commentary on certain key issues in the draft see T. Green 'Reflections on the People of God Schema' in *Proceedings of the Fortieth Annual Convention of the Canon Law Society of America* (1978) 13-33.

5. *Acta Apostolicae Sedis* 58 (1966) 757-787 (henceforth referred to as *AAS*).

6. *Communicationes* 1 (1969) 77-100.

7. F. Klostermann 'Reform of Church Structures' in *Rethinking the Church (La fine della Chiesa come societa perfetta)* ed. M. Cuminetti and F. V. Johannes (Dublin 1970) pp. 142-193 esp. 142-156.

8. For a detailed examination of various theological-canonical issues arising from the Code revision process see T. Green 'The Revision of Canon Law: Theological Implications' *Theological Studies* 40 (1979) 593-679 (henceforth cited as Green, 'Revision . . .').

9. Interestingly enough the first Code Commission report on the reworking of the *De Populo Dei* draft indicates that a significant part of the section on the basic obligations and rights of believers has been dropped since the issues are dealt with in the *Lex*. (*Communicationes* 12 (1980) 77-91.)

10. The *Coetus* on Physical and Juridical Persons is responsible for the norms on physical persons (2-15) and on juridical persons (70-80). The *Coetus* on the Laity and Associations of the Faithful articulated the norms in three new sections of the schema: the basic obligations and rights of believers (16-38), associations of the Christian faithful (39-69) and the Christian laity (523-533). The *Coetus* on the Magisterium prepared the norms on the formation of clerics (81-119), formerly treated in Book III of the Code in the section on the magisterium. Finally the *Coetus* on the Sacred Hierarchy formulated the rest of the norms in the schema.

11. For a more detailed examination of the implications of the principles for the reform of the Code in its entirety see Green 'Revision . . .' 627-668.

12. *Ibid.* 630-641.

13. These issues are examined in greater detail by Professor Komonchak in the preceding article in this issue.

14. Green 'Revision . . .' 641-648.

15. *AAS* 57 (1965) 775-780.

16. Sacra Congregatio pro Episcopis *Directorium de Pastorali Ministerio Episcoporum* (Typis Polyglottis Vaticanis 1973).

17. Green 'Revision . . .' 648-651.

18. *AAS* 62 (1970) 459-465.

19. Green 'Revision . . .' 656-668.

20. *AAS* 58 (1966) 467-471.

E

Herwi Rikhof

The Ecclesiologies of *Lumen gentium,* the *Lex Ecclesiae Fundamentalis* and the Draft Code

1. PRELIMINARY PROBLEMS

THIS ARTICLE is concerned with ecclesiology as it appears in the three basic texts for this revision of canon law: *Lumen gentium* (LG), the *Lex Ecclesiae Fundamentalis* (LEF), and the draft of the new *Codex Iuris Canonici* (SCIC). But the critical examination of these three texts from this angle presents two problems, the first connected with the difference in character and language between the three; the second concerns LG.

The first problem lies in that LG was partly a reaction against the legal slant which, before, had coloured so much ecclesial thinking and language. This means that the comparison must show the differences in thought and language as they appear in the three texts. The fact that LEF and SCIC are supposed to have translated Vatican II into legal terms carries an implication which may help to cope with this problem. The fact that one moves from one level of thinking and speaking has two consequences for the way in which one should compare these texts.

The first point is that it is really impossible to compare the texts simply by putting them side by side. The juridical texts have to be traced back to their origin; the underlying view of the Church has to be reconstrued from structural indications, scraps of theology, and so on. Here the way LEF got off the ground could be very illuminating because the earlier drafts show a mixture of theological and legal expressions, while, as in SCIC, the last version shows a preference for more juridical ways of expression. Thus the LEF could have the kind of bridging function which historically fits the rôle it plays in the whole process of producing a revision of canon law. Consequently, the crux and the criterion of collation and assessment lie in LG, the dogmatic Constitution, because the other texts obviously are interpretations of the Constitution. But this means that we have to face a second problem, and that is precisely LG.

If the term 'ecclesiology' is meant to refer to a coherent and straightforward understanding of the Church, LG shows no such simple and straightforward ecclesiology. The vision of the Church which it displays is full of elements and fragments which are either contradictory or open to various explanations. This requires an

54

evaluation of the LG's own view of the Church, and so complicates the comparison between it and the other two texts. So what has to be done is not simply to establish where LEF and SCIC correspond to LG but to evaluate such a correspondence in the light of those points of ecclesiology revealed by such a correspondence. In other words, one has to find out whether LEF and SCIC show the same pluralistic view of the Church as LG, and if not, whether this passage from the pluralistic to a more uniform view constitutes progress or not. This issue gives a further dimension to the questions whether LEF and SCIC show that a great opportunity has been missed.

All this shows that our investigation should proceed in three stages: first, we must see which various ecclesiological elements are contained in LG and how we should judge them; then we must find out which of these elements are maintained in the earlier version of LEF, and finally we must look at the final version of LEF and SCIC in the light of the previous part of this investigation.

Because of the problems mentioned before, less attention will be paid to the SCIC and the main burden of the argument will inevitably lie in the significance of LEF. But since LEF provided a kind of framework for the SCIC, and both had therefore the same basic approach, this SCIC is implied in the discussion, though more indirectly.

2. THE CONCEPT OF THE CHURCH IN LG[1]

At first sight the final text of LG seems to differ on all relevant issues from the first schema. The procedure is different: the place of the chapter on the people of God has been changed; the approach is different: chapter I is now entitled 'The Mystery of the Church' instead of 'The Nature of the Church Militant', and another expression is used as a basic pointer: people of God, instead of the mystical body of Christ. But a closer look reveals no radical break. The best way of showing that apart from this discontinuity there persisted a definite continuity is best shown by tracing the historical origin of the first two chapters. These are decisive for the concept of the Church as a whole and therefore determine the crux and the criterion we need for the comparison.

The first schema suffered the same fate as most other schemata produced by the preparatory commission: it was rejected and disqualified as too clericalist, triumphalist and legalistic. The central concept in this schema was 'the mystical body of Christ'. The way in which this image was used there showed quite clearly that the principal concern of this schema turned on the identification of the social element (*societas*) with the inward element (*corpus mysticum*), and in this identification the analogy with the incarnation played a crucial part. This identification was used as the basic justification for the thesis that the Church professed in the creed and the Roman Catholic Church were one and the same and that the word 'Church' could therefore only apply to this Roman Catholic Church. The next point of essential importance is then that this 'body' was interpreted as consisting of members who are 'in no sense equal'. This implies that the Church consists of two groups with a vast difference in status: the one is subject to the other. In formulating this difference in status much use was made of the three functions attributed to Christ as priest, king and teacher which are reserved to the hierarchy. Another vital point is that this identification makes the Church the final term. This is clear from the way in which salvation history is treated, which in this text consists of two phrases: God's plan to save all men collectively and the fulfilment of that plan in the Church which is taught, sanctified and governed by Jesus (himself and through the specially chosen leaders). Thus the Church becomes an end in itself, which, in fact, leaves no room for salvation history.

This whole schema was really an attempt to continue the ideas contained in the encyclical *Mystici Corporis*. This encyclical tried to reconcile two divergent views of the Church: the limited apologetic and rather legalistic approach from the angle of an ecclesiology of the *societas* and the 'mystical' approach of the various ecclesiologies derived from the concept of the 'mystical body'. The encylical attempted this on the basis of the rejected schema *De Ecclesia* of Vatican I, which made the legalistic view the framework within which the other approach should be worked out. This in fact implies that the interpretation of the Church on the basis of: 'the Church is the mystical body of Christ', proceeds from 'the Church' to 'the mystical body of Christ'. The way the encylical interprets 'body' and 'of Christ' reveals that it started with an assumed view of the Church which saw the Church as the institution which absolutely guaranteed the 'depositum fidei' entrusted to it. This statement allows the Church to refer to Christ who founded the Church with a constitution which neither needs nor can allow for any alteration simply because this Church is the continuation of Christ. This interpretation stresses the independence of the Church in so far as people are concerned. This, in turn, necessarily leads to a one-way traffic in communication: the overriding sanctity of the institutional Church is in no way diminished by the sinfulness of the people, and with this, the Church is constantly teaching the people who are reduced to the status of mere listeners. All this implies that the Church is simply prised out of history since history implies change, relativity and consequently doubt.[2]

The second schema started from a combination of the rejected one with elements of a fresh approach. A number of drafts led to this second schema, an analysis of which shows a gradual convergence of the two approaches. This new attempt, for instance, shows that more attention was paid to salvation history, eschatology, the rôle of the Spirit, as well as to a more extensive use of such terms as 'mystery', 'sacrament' and 'germ and origin'. The Church is no longer the end-product but has become, so to speak, more transparent because it allows one to see through it to what it is the sacrament, germ and origin of, namely, union with God and the unity of all mankind, in other words, the kingdom of God.

Since these opposite approaches are here concurrently at work this schema is charged with a constant tension. It wants to maintain the exclusive claim to 'the Church' while recognising that the sanctifying process is going on outside the Roman Catholic Church, the two phases of salvation history go together with respect for the rôle of the Spirit.

There is also an inconsistent use of the term 'mystical body': it is used both to describe the inner and outward aspects of the unity of the Church, but through the analogy with the incarnation it is also used to express exclusively the unity of the divine and the inward aspects. The same tension shows in the way the expression 'people of God' is taken: understood in its biblical sense this expression is now given a more prominent place, and yet, it is also given a more limited sense when referring to 'a group of people'.

The third schema reinforces the new approach. This shows in the whole structure of the text, firstly, in that it has implemented the earlier decision to devote a separate chapter to the Church as the people of God and to place it before the chapter on the hierarchy; secondly, within the first chapter salvation history is linked with the work of the Trinity so that it is no longer limited to just two phases; and, thirdly, a new section has been added on the kingdom of God. The process works through in individual numbers since the exclusive uncompromising use of 'is' has been enlarged by replacing this verb by 'subsists in' (*subsistit*). All this, however, does not mean that the old approach has completely disappeared. For instance, LG § 8, which goes back to the central piece of the first scheme, contains elements taken from that old approach: it identifies the hierarchically organised society with the mystical body ('a complex reality') and keeps the analogy with the incarnation. And while in LG § 7 the expression 'mystical body' is given a biblical interpretation, the term remains ambivalent in chapter I, which, for instance, still argues that this is a central concept because it is more than an image and provides a deeper insight into the mystery of the Church. Nor is it clear how the two dominant expressions (and the first two chapters) are related. This surely shows that the new approach has not been thought through in all its consequences and has not been clearly worked out in the text.

To evaluate these various elements and approaches we need a formal framework of systematic ecclesiology which shows the boundaries within which one can meaningfully think and speak about the Church, and provides the elements which should be argued.[3] This can be worked out if we start from a basic meaning which will point to the opening which will in turn lead to what is the hall-mark of ecclesiology. If there is no such specific opening, then ecclesiology has no claim to being a separate theological discipline: it could, for instance, be reduced to Christology. The collective aspect of the faith is such an opening and 'the Church is the communion of the faithful' provides such a basic meaning. Formally understood, this meaning primarily indicates the relation with God, Father, Son and Spirit, and that this relation is constitutive; it also implies that one can argue about how this relation works out in practice, but it shows that a view of the Church in terms of God, Father, Son and Spirit would not fit in and is excluded. In other words, there is meaning in a *Christo-centric* approach, but not in a purely *Christological* one.

Moreover, this basic meaning also points to the fact that the aspects of time and space which are typical of the human community are therefore also well within the borders of the ecclesiological framework. It therefore becomes necessary that such an ecclesiology should include history, form, function and structure. This implies that there is a point in arguing about change, about sacrament(s), hierarchical or synodal structures. But it becomes meaningless to take an a-historical, invisible and unstructured Church seriously. In so far as LG is concerned this means that the old approach must be admitted to be largely incoherent because it puts the Church outside and above history and because it is dominated by the delusion of the spurious problem of 'visible' and 'invisible'.

The old approach showed indeed some interest in structures but if these are seen outside the historical context this also becomes obviously incoherent; moreover, the concrete structure is put forward as 'willed by God' and so systematically escapes any proper argument. This old approach was 'Christological' rather than 'Christo-centric' and this makes it incoherent because we are not dealing with Christology but with ecclesiology. In principle, the new approach can be deemed to be 'coherent'. Where the final text of LG creates problems is where the discussion to which it gave rise led to such points as whether the Church was Christo-centric, or pneumato-centric, or whatever. In so far as this investigation is concerned this last remark is of less importance because the real point at issue is which approach was adopted by LEF and SCIC.

3. THE *LEX ECCLESIAE FUNDAMENTALIS*[4]

Although the last version of the LEF (1976) contains less 'theological' texts than the version of 1970, it is not wholly without. The canons which introduce the two main parts consist of (modified) parts of canons which revealed the theological approach in the earlier version. Apart from the problem mentioned before, these older and longer texts are important because although these texts are gone the vision has not, and because they give a more complete picture of that vision.[5]

(a) The Prooemium or Preface

This Preface to the whole text of LEF is made up of three paragraphs, and the central concept which runs through all three is that of 'mission'. In the first paragraph the Father sends Christ; in the second Christ founds a Church to carry on his mission, and in the third the Church is said to accomplish this mission through its laws, among other ways. The first two paragraphs refer to LG §§ 1, 2, 4, 8 and 9. A careful check reveals that words and parts of sentences have indeed been taken from the numbers referred to but that there are important differences resulting from a different combination or putting things in a different context. Salvation history, extensively treated in LG § 1, has here been reduced to two phases mentioned above (the fulfillment of 'God's plan') as part of schema 1. The Church has lost its transparent character. The subtlety of the way differences occur is sometimes so cunning as to produce a smile on a detective's face. There is the case of a simple change of grammatical case: LG says that God had decided to bring men together 'in ecclesia' (ablative)—this implies that people accept God's invitation and so grow as a Church'. But LEF uses tha accusative, 'in ecclesiam', and this means direction towards an outside end, as if the Church is a kind of reality which exists independently of the actual faithful who make it up (paragraph 1).

Paragraph 2 says that Christ 'established his holy Church, which he intended as a community of faith, hope and charity in the world, in the shape of a hierarchically organised society'. This one sentence is a combination of two sentences from LG § 8: 'Christ, the one Mediator, established . . . here on earth His Holy Church, the community of faith, hope and charity, as a visible structure' and 'but the society furnished with hierarchical agencies and the Mystical Body of Christ are not to be considered as two realities'. The second sentence of LG indeed follows on the first, but here the contraction is too abrupt: one sentence talks about 'community', the other about 'society', two very different levels.[6] This contraction of the two sentences of LG into one by LEF shows that LEF is going back to the dominant theme of schema 1 (last sentence): the dominant category is *societas* and the hierarchical structure is attributed to Christ. Then it is asserted that this hierarchical society must be a 'sacrament'. This is a combination which at least shows a change of emphasis in so far as LG §§ 1 and 9 are concerned. Even the transition from paragraph 1 to paragraph 2 shows the old approach: '*therefore* Christ founded his Church'. The new approach saw Christ rather as inaugurating the kingdom (LG §§ 3 and 5) and the Holy Spirit as playing a constitutive part in the formation of the Church (LG § 4, a text which is indeed referred to but has not been used).

The most important part of paragraph 3 does not bother to give any source at all. But the formulae reveal a self-confidence ('the Church fulfils its mission') which is out of tune with the sense of weakness and of guilt which LG so humbly reveals, and they also show a defensive attitude ('the Church maintains and protects its God-imposed structure uncompromisingly'). This cannot but recall the triumphalistic and apologetic accents of schema 1.

Another indication that the authors of LEF read LG with the pre-conciliar ecclesiology in terms of *societas* in mind shows in the inconsistencies implied in their use of *societas* and *communitas*. If the whole point was to make room for the law in the Church (which was the explicitly stated purpose of the commission) the expressions *communitas* or *societas* would have served the purpose without any further qualification. This is recognised in the *relatio* where it refers to the adage: *ubi societas, ibi ius*. But this is clearly not the main intent of this introduction; it is rather meant to show that a hierarchical structure is something which is obvious from the start. This is why the term *societas* is used as the more obviously appropriate one.

(i) *Chapter I: Church or people of God (cc. 1 and 2)*

Chapter 1 deals with the nature (the priesthood of all born of the water and the Spirit), purpose (the kingdom of God) and structure (the institution of ministers by

Christ). Paragraph 1 briefly mentions the purpose but concentrates on the notion of 'Church'. Here use is made, first of all, of some terms in pairs: body of Christ—people of God, spiritual community—hierarchical society. Then two series of terms are used which are coupled with the divine and the human element. This is clearly inspired by the discussion about the visible and invisible Church and the analogy with the incarnation. This angle, so typical of schema 1, has been preserved in LG § 8, and LEF refers to it. This explains a change from LEF (1969): there the expression *Christi ecclesia* was used which here has become *Corpus Christi, quod est ecclesia*. This new formulation shows strong associations with the pre-conciliar theology of the mystical body. This change has rather important consequences. The single dominant concept of 'people of God' was broken up: the two expressions 'body of Christ' and 'people of God' now appear side by side while the parallel with community and society now strongly suggests that the 'body of Christ' stands for the inward spiritual reality while 'people of God' stands for the external aspect. This is confirmed by the observation in the *relatio* that this addition was made because the notion of the Church as the mystical(!) body is a richer image than any other and because it is a better expression of the mystery of Christ. This means that not only do we find here again the unclarified relation between people of God and body of Christ, but also that the ambivalent way in which these terms were understood has been brought back into use. The observation made in the *relatio* shows that the text is not really concerned with the mystery of the Church but with the mystery of Christ.

While paragraph 2 (nature) indeed refers to that part of LG § 10 which deals with the universal priesthood, paragraph 3 (structure) refers to the part of LG § 10 which stresses the difference between the universal priesthood and the official one. This is brought about by the use of terms and ideas which already occur in schema 1 and are used again in LEF: 'sacra potestas', 'in persona Christi', implying the exclusively Christological foundation of the ministry.

In the description of the office one recognises the three functions of Christ. Moreover, the fact that there are also references here to the chapter on the hierarchy (LG §§ 21, 24 and 27, though without quotations) gives the impression that these three functions, which in chapter II of LG are attributed to the whole people of God, are here reserved to the hierarchy, as was usual before LG. Paragraph 4 deals with the unity of the people and the rôle of the Spirit. It refers to LG §§ 4 and 13. Fragments taken from these sections have been condensed into one sentence, and this reveals a number of changes. The fragment from LG § 4 states that it is the Spirit which makes the Church one in community and service; this is left out of our text. On the other hand, there appears an addition which states that the Spirit equips the Church in an 'ordered manner' with charismatic and hierarchical gifts. These changes fit in with the trend shown in paragraph 3. The context of the fragment taken from LG § 13 states that the mission of the Spirit is on the same level as that of the Son, but there is no trace of this in our paragraph.

Chapter 2 treats of the oneness and the pluralism of the Church and raises several important issues. Paragraph 1 speaks of the Church as based on one creed and existing (*existit*) in, as well as made up of, particular churches. It quotes fragments from LG § 8 and links up with observations from LG § 23. The fragments introduce the new 'subsistit'. In connection with that 'subsistit' LG § 8 makes a subtle distinction between Peter and the apostles on the one hand and the successor of Peter with his bishops on the other. This 'subsistit' and this distinction have vanished from our present text. On the contrary, through the combination of this with the part which deals with the relations obtaining in the 'College of Bishops' the Church of the creed becomes identical with the Roman Catholic Church, which exists in the particular churches of which it is made up.

It is worth noting that in dealing with the various ways in which the particular churches work out the apostolic heritage in practice (paragraph 3), the text refers to a passage from the Decree on Ecumenism (UR § 14, on Eastern Christians). There the diversity is linked with character and life-style but is looked at in a neutral or even negative way. But LG § 11 saw this bond in a positive light—yet, LG § 11 has not been used in our text. This eclectic treatment fits in with a view of the Church which sees the human element as a harmful influence. The same may be said of the way in which paragraph 4 tackles the question of the need for constant reform (LG § 8): this is not linked with the weakness of the Church and its members but with the unity between particular churches and with 'inaccuracies which have crept in'.

(ii) *Chapter II: the functions of the Church (cc. 51 and 53)*

In c. 51, 1, the connection between the mission of the Church and its functions is introduced by way of a comparison: just as the Father sent Christ, teacher, king and priest, so Christ has transmitted this three-fold task to the Twelve in order to continue the Church. These functions are briefly worked out in paragraph 2. The common source of these two paragraphs is LG § 5, but there are differences. LG § 5 relates the Church to the kingdom of God and this has been added in the last version. The initial statement that the mystery of the Church is made manifest in its foundation is worked out in two points.

Jesus inaugurated the Church by proclaiming the kingdom of God in his word, his deeds and his personal presence. After his death and resurrection he poured out the Spirit on his disciples, and thus the Church received its mission, namely, to proclaim the kingdom. The Church is the germ and the beginning of that kingdom. Paragraph 1 does not make this distinction between Church and kingdom, and by using the expression 'aedificare ecclesiam' (instead of 'fundatio') and 'stabiliri ecclesiam' seems to do away with the relativity of the Church. Moreover, the Twelve are not seen as prefiguration of the messianic people of God but as the first bishops consecrated by Jesus. The rôle of the Spirit is reduced to this ordination, in contrast to LG §§ 5 and 13, although these passages are referred to.

Paragraph 2 does indeed mention the kingdom and gives more prominence to the rôle of the Spirit, but it is seen here as additional rather than as constitutive: LEF (1970) indeed has added a clause which manages to bring in the distinction between hierarchy and laity ('with different gifts of the Holy Spirit according to the difference of the members'—see the observations made in connection with c. 1, 1). The description of the tasks of the Church refers to a section of the chapter on the people of God, LG § 16 (dealing with non-Christians, though LG § 17, on the missionary function would have been more obviously apt), and to two sections from the chapter on the hierarchy (LG §§ 26 and 27). LG § 27, however, offers no support for the description of the 'governing' function. This section of LG makes service, ministry, the main theme. It is therefore curious that this central theme has not been incorporated in our text.

These references and textual modifications reveal the tension underlying this canon. At first sight one already notices this tension when passing from paragraph 1 to paragraph 2: 1 makes the Church the final term while 2 makes it the kingdom of God; 1 limits the church *de facto* to the bishops, while 2 concerns the whole Church. This tension is tightened by the opposition between the various additions to this version.

The *relatio* states that the remark about the various gifts of the Spirit has been added in order to emphasise the fact that this is a matter involving the whole Church, and yet, it also states that the word *consecravit* has been added to make clear the division between the universal and the official priesthood. If one takes the primary and declared intent of the commission seriously, one becomes aware of an even greater tension: the delineation of the three functions of the Church suits only the hierarchy and does not concern the people of God as a whole. The very description of the function of government ('that all belonging to the people of God may be led') shows the fact that it is assumed that we have here a two-tier system and an opposition between the two. In itself it is possible to ascribe the power of government to people as a whole (conceptually and in fact) but this implies one or other form of democracy, where all members can make their contribution. But this is not recognisable in the canons which cover this function of government. These state in fact that the Church must 'lead' the faithful, and for this purpose it is said to have complete power (legislative, executive and judicial), which is in the hands of the ministers appointed by God (c. 75), and that the highest and most complete level belongs to the pope and the College of Bishops (c. 76; see c. 79, 2 and 3).

The description of the other functions has been given the same treatment. It would have been possible to leave the chapter on the hierarchy alone and to refer instead to the second chapter, to LG § 10 about the universal priesthood, to LG § 12 about the sense of faith (*sensus fidelium*), which starts by stating that the people of God share in Christ's prophetic office, and to LG § 17, already mentioned above. Canon 53, 3 refers to LG §§ 10 and 12, and states that those who believe in Christ share in Christ's three functions but *suo modo*, in their own way. The structure of this canon (paragraph 1, the bishops; paragraph 2, the priests and deacons; paragraph 3, the faithful—see c. 65) and the way it is formulated (*principally* the bishops, *also* the priests, and the faithful *in their own way*) show the subordinate position of this statement in the overall view and imply that the faithful of paragraph 3 are in fact the laity. If this is the case, then the *suo modo* can only be taken as adequately conveying the meaning of LG if it really means an active and specific contribution by the laity. Unfortunately, c. 83 makes it quite plain that in matters of government the laity's contribution *suo modo* consists in carrying out what the bishop has ordered, while c. 62 distinguishes between proclaiming the gospel 'privately' and in the name of the Church, which is rather damning in this particular context. So the *bonum fidei* (the treasury of the faith) remains after all the exclusive property of the bishops (c. 54; see the use of 'proprii' in c. 71).

All this brings us face to face with the use of doctrine of *munera*, the teaching about the functions, in ecclesiology. Originally it was a help in sorting out Christology. But the attempt to deal with this section of theology by introducing the three-fold function of Christ was in the nineteenth century transferred to ecclesiology, and when the ministry was interpreted in terms of Christ's functions this three-fold model ousted the traditional division of the functions of the Church into two parts, the power of jurisdiction and the power of order (*potestas iurisdictionis* and *potestas ordinis*).[7] In principle LG severed this link with the theology of function and office, and attributed Christ's function to the people of God as a whole, but it failed to work out the far-reaching and radical conceptual and actual consequences of this interpretation. To do this would require a thorough overhaul of the theology of office and function, of the teaching on infallibility, and so on. LEF nowhere shows any sign of such a reconstruction or of even translating this statement of principle in LG into legal terms. The extension mentioned in c. 53, 3, seems to be a mere formality.

4. CONCLUSION

Analysis, comparison and the various observations clearly show that LEF (1970) has consistently opted for those elements in LG which were retained from the old approach of schema 1, and against those elements in it of the new approach which, though not completely thought through on every point, nevertheless differs fundamentally and in principle from that of schema 1. The critical evaluation of the two approaches leads to the conclusion that, although LEF shows greater consistency and less complexity, it is not a move forward but rather a relapse into the old incoherent ecclesiology. The question now remains whether the later version of LEF and SCIC suggest a different conclusion.

(a) The *Lex Ecclesiae Fundamentalis* (1976)[8]

(i) *Part I: the Church*

Chapter 1 deals with the unicity of the Church and its God-willed division into two levels or classes. Compared with earlier texts this particular text shows changes which at first sight seem contradictory. Paragraph 1 has picked up the 'subsistit' alteration, mentioned above, but the people of God have vanished from paragraph 2. This means that the fundamental description of the Church as the people of God, before any other distinctions are introduced, has disappeared (see also the titles of the parts of this text), and that the division into two tiers or classes has taken its place. But in this context 'subsistit' does not indicate a divergence from the old approach. In LG § 8 the use of the verb 'subsistit' implies that there are differences between the Church of the creed and the Roman Catholic Church, and therefore, that there are issues where the Roman Catholic Church is subject to criticism by the Church of the creed. One will expect this kind of conflict to appear in the area described in the creed by the so-called four 'notes' of the Church: unity, sanctity, apostolicity and catholicity.

It is essential to realise that we are here concerned with formulae which as part of the creed and because of the place given them there (I believe in the Holy Spirit) are definitely not superficial statements about existing conditions but ways of expressing the eschatological statement: 'this is all—but not yet'. This means that the four 'notes' must be seen as directives for communal conduct and as norms which the community must constantly aim at (and actually achieves from time to time). They should not be seen as the official qualities which one group can claim as its inalienable possession. Unfortunately, LEF only sees the four 'notes' in this latter sense. It reduces 'apostolicity' to apostolic succession, which then also becomes the exclusive criterion for unicity and oneness.[9] It has a peculiar interpretation of sanctity, where the need for constant reform is used in the same irrelevant way as in the previous version. It finally shows in the self-confidence which takes for granted that the Church of the creed 'is present, operates and grows' in the particular churches.

(ii) *Part II: the Church's functions (cc. 55-56)*

Canon 55 is a very simplified version of previous canons. It contains, however, a new element: the function of government is here entrusted with responsibility for all the other functions. This makes this function the seat of power (in the crude sense). This of course reinforces the two-class system of c. 1 and government becomes again the focal point. Canon 56 makes no bones about the two-class system: the earlier version only suggested that the *suo modo* only applied to the laity, but here it is spelt out in detail and structure. So we have paragraph 1 dealing with bishops, priests and deacons, while paragraph 2 designs to look at the laity. Paragraph 3 then states that, because of their baptism and confirmation, the laity are actually fit to receive particular charges or functions from the hierarchy. This way of putting things shows not only that baptism and confirmation simply acknowledge an aptitude, not a basic right, but also that all these functions are the exclusive preserve of the hierarchy, and they can farm them out as they see fit (see c. 80). References to the *sensus fidelium* and the universal priesthood have disappeared. The laity have once again been reduced to the status of 'subjects' (see c. 12), and the area where they operate is again put outside what one may call in this context 'Church territory', in so far as temporal and 'worldly' matters are concerned (cc. 50 and 51; see c. 28, 2). These canons clearly see the Church as detached from people and humanity. It has nothing to do with culture, politics, economics or social issues. This, of course, perfectly suits a concept of the Church which believes in the class-system (clergy and laity) and in the one-way traffic.

The way in which the commission chose and picked its way through previous theological texts and too revealing changes of approach makes it quite obvious that the authors opted for the ecclesiology in terms of 'society' which was current before the Council.

(b) The SCIC draft (1980)

All that has been said so far makes it unnecessary to spend a lot of time and space on SCIC. Both the structure and the content of the most important canons show the same view of the Church as LEF. The overruling dominance of the government as shown in LEF is here continued by putting it under the general norms of Book I. Moreover, the term 'munus' is no longer used but replaced by the 'potestas' of old, while the *potestas regiminis* is equated with *potestas iurisdictionis*, and simply subdivided into legislative, executive and judicial power (cc. 126 and 132). It is true that the doctrine of the *munera* partly determines the structure of the code, but, because the 'suo modo' of all the faithful is determined by the juridical status (c. 201) and therefore by the basic bipartite division of the Church (c. 202), it is clear that the broadening of the concept in LG has not really been accepted: the laity are at most co-operators of the hierarchy and the scope of their responsibility lies outside the Church (see, for instance, cc. 270, 277, 711, etc.). The general conclusion therefore has to be that LEF and SCIC are definitely retrograde and not merely a missed opportunity.

Translated by T. L. Westow

Notes

1. For an extensive analysis, see H. Rikhof *The Concept of Church*. A methodological inquiry into the use of metaphors in ecclesiology (London/Sheperdstown 1981) chapter 1.

2. See also R. Ardelt 'Anmerkungen zur antimodernistischen Ekklesiologie' *Der Modernismus* ed. E. Weinzierl (Graz/Vienna/Cologne 1974) pp. 257-282.

3. For this paragraph see H. Rikhof, the book cited in note 1, chapter 4.

4. The text of LEF (1976) has appeared in translation in *Herder Korrespondenz* 32 (1978), col. 632 ff. LEF (1969 and 1970) can be found, with the *relationes* in G. Alberigo (and others) in *Legge e Vangelo* (Brescia 1972) pp. 491-657.

5. In what follows I have brought out the main points while the references to LG have been checked and commented upon. It is not always clear why a given section of LG has been referred to (as in c. 1, 1 referring to LG § 48; c. 51, 2 to LG § 16). These references have therefore been ignored. The same has happened with c. 2, 1 (a literal quote of LG § 23) and c. 52, because the main source there is the Decree on the Liturgy.

6. See the *nota praevia* which formally indicates the structural aspect of the community.

7. See P. Persson *Repraesentatio Christi* (Göttingen 1966).

8. The relevant canons of LEF (1976) are based on the following canons of LEF (1970): 1, 1 on 2, 1; 1, 2 on 1, 3; 2, 1 on 2, 1; 2, 2 on 2, 2; 2, 4 on 2, 4; 50, 1 on 1, 1; 50, 2 on 85, 1; 51, 1 on 85, 2; 51, 2 on 87, 2; 55, 1 on 51, 2; 55, 2 on 52; 56, 1 on 53, 1-2; 56, 2 on 53, 3.

9. For its formulation LEF has here opted for LG § 18 where there is a reference to Vatican I. In LG § 13 the Spirit is called the foundation, but this has not been used.

Aelred Cody

The New Canons on Consecrated Life and the Mind of the Council

ON 2 February 1977, the subcommission to which the Pontifical Commission for the Revision of the Code of Canon Law had entrusted the task of drafting the canons on institutes of perfection (as they were called in 1966) finished its draft of those canons, by then called 'Canons on Institutes of Life Consecrated by the Profession of the Evangelical Counsels' and sent it to dicasteries of the Roman Curia, episcopal conferences, ecclesiastical faculties, superiors general of the institutes concerned, and some groups of nuns, for comments and suggestions. Six preliminary canons were followed by a First Part with eighty-two general canons applicable to every type of consecrated life, and then by a Second Part with thirty-eight canons in which institutes were distinguished typologically, with specific legislation made for each type. There were many negative reactions, and the religious superiors consulted expressed a general dissatisfaction which amounted to a rejection of the draft as it stood, although many of its details were found to be laudable. The criticisms were of various kinds. Some rose from desire for more clarity or from practical problems foreseen in following the provisions of certain canons. Others rose from questions of principle. A new subcommission, a number of whose members had been members of the earlier one, was then formed, with a mandate to revise and emend the 1977 draft, taking account of the comments received. By the summer of 1980 the revised text was finished and sent to the cardinals who are members of the Pontifical Commission for the Revision of the Code. Any reservations and emendations received from them are to be discussed in a plenary session of the Commission, and the final text will then be submitted to the pope.

To what extent did the draft of 1977 reflect the mind of the Fathers of the Second Vatican Council or depart from that mind, and to what extent has the revised text of 1980 brought the legislation closer to that mind?

1. OBJECTIVELY AND SUBJECTIVELY DIFFERENT VIEWPOINTS

Perhaps no other subcommission has shown so strong a desire to express in the legislation of the new Code positions taken in documents of the Council. Many phrases used in the canons of the 1977 draft were actually drawn from Chapter VI of the dogmatic constitution *Lumen gentium* (henceforth: LG) or from the decree *Perfectae caritatis* (henceforth: PC). Comparisons of the new canons with the documents of the Second Vatican Council may, like all comparisons, be odious when judgments of value are involved. Those conciliar documents which dealt with religious have themselves been criticised. While the 1977 draft was criticised for including secular institutes in its legislation for religious, Chapter VI of LG has been criticised for omitting secular institutes from its consideration of the place and rôle of religious in the Church. If many criticised Part I of the 1977 draft for reducing all religious to a common denominator which was that of the secular institute, others have criticised the conciliar documents for taking too monastic and conventual a view of all religious. The prescription of the draft's canon 14, retained in the new canon 505 § 2, that it belongs to the 'competent ecclesiastical authority . . . to interpret the evangelical counsels, regulate their practice by laws, and by canonical approval erect stable forms for living by them' has been criticised for being too juridical to be faithful to what is said of the evangelical counsels in LG §§ 42, 44 and 46 and PC §§ 5 and 6, but to be fair one must also say that it does represent the mind, and in fact much of the language, of LG §§ 43 and 45.

One problem with which one must reckon in assessing the fidelity of the canons of the new code to the documents of the Council lies in the fact that the conciliar documents, though directive, deal with religious primarily in theological and spiritual terms, while the canons of the Code have to deal with persons and societies in terms which are primarily legal and juridical. Law contains norms of action, while theological and spiritual directives contain norms of thought or of ideology. On several occasions Pope Paul VI, mindful of some criticisms of the *Codex Iuris Canonici* of 1917, called upon the members of the Commission for the new Code to keep its legislation based on sound doctrine and close to sane theology. On the other hand, the first of the ten norms governing the new codification insisted that the new Code was to be a juridical document regulating the rights and obligations of individuals to one another and to society as a whole (see *Communicationes* 2 (1969) 77-85). This does not positively exclude material stating theological or spiritual principles, and the members of the subcommission for the canons on religious incorporated far more doctrinal material in their draft than did those of any other subcommission. In doing so, they meant to carry conciliar principles into post-conciliar legislation, but the resulting mixture of ideological principles with juridical prescriptions exposed the draft to negative reactions from people with quite different points of view. Those who expect a code to be consistently juridical, although doctrinally based, found all the hortatory material in the 1977 draft out of place and somewhat unprofessional, while those who somehow expected the new Code to be as theological and spiritual as possible were not only displeased by the juridical tone of many canons but tended in many cases to disagree with the ideological principles expressed in many canons—often on grounds of departure from the mind of Vatican II. Of the draft's purely doctrinal canon 3, for example, retained as canon 505 § 1 of the revised *schema*, which states that the evangelical counsels are based on the doctrine and examples of Christ and are a divine gift received by the Church from God and kept by his grace, one superior general, referring to LG § 42, said that the canon ought to be placed in a more Christological, spiritual, historical, and ecclesial perspective, while a national conference of major superiors thought that it should be completely removed from the Code because it was homiletic and verbose, and out of place in a legal code.

The new subcommission, while recognising the place of doctrinal material, especially in the first four canons of the common norms, has made the legal prescriptions more consistently juridical. In the 1977 draft, canon 44, giving the absolute requirements for admission to any type of institute, included the requisite that the person seeking admission be 'endowed with a divine vocation'. In the emended text of 1980 (canon 524) this is changed to read 'endowed with a right intention'. The change illustrates well the different approach of the revisors to questions of theology in matters of regulation. It is not the approach characteristically found in the conciliar documents, but those documents were not meant to provide the norms for dealing with concrete situations necessary in a code.

2. ALTERATIONS OF CONCILIAR MODELS

More serious were the accusations that the framers of the 1977 draft deformed the intentions expressed in conciliar documents. It would be unfair and unjust to attribute exaggeratedly tendentious motives to the framers of the draft, but such accusations of having deformed the mind of the Council Fathers were in some cases justified. They could be made with respect to what was in the judgment of many persons one of the major defects of the draft: the typological classification of different kinds of specifically religious institutes in Part II, with the uniform and levelling nature of the legislation for all types of institutes in the general canons of Part I. The basis of the typological distinctions was set down in canon 89 § 1 of the 1977 draft. Much of this canon's text is taken *verbatim* from LG § 46's exhortation of religious to show to the world 'Christ contemplating on the mountain, or announcing the kingdom of God to the multitudes, or healing the ill and the wounded and converting sinners into good fruit, or blessing children, and doing good to all', but that series is not restrictive, it is not at all meant as a typological description of all religious institutes on the basis of activity, and it does not include the words of the canon designed to apply to secular institutes. The passage of LG was used, with alteration, for purposes going beyond those intended by the Council. The 1980 *schema* retains this canon, as canon 506, but the revisors, as we shall see, have given it the function which is in fact that of LG § 46.

The typological classification of institutes undertaken by the Council itself is found in PC §§ 7-11: contemplative religious institutes (PC § 7), religious institutes devoted to various forms of the apostolate (PC § 8), monastic religious institutes (PC § 9), and secular institutes, expressly said not to be religious institutes (PC § 11); an institute of any of these categories may be either clerical or lay, but PC § 10 speaks of lay institutes in general. According to PC § 1, that entire decree was meant to provide general principles for the renewal of *religious* institutes (i.e., those whose members profess vows juridically recognised as 'public' and have common life), although they were to be applicable also to societies of common life without public vows and to secular institutes, as long as neither category lost its special character. The inclusion of secular institutes in the first place was the result of a late compromise made before the final Session of the Council; it worked well enough in PC because PC was not a juridical document. The inclusion of secular institutes in PC was the model of their inclusion in the new Code, but while PC made it clear that they were not religious institutes, the codifiers of the 1977 draft framed the general canons of Part I in such a way that they might almost be called laws for *secular* institutes, meant to be observed also by religious and by members of societies of common life without public vows. Such terms as 'profession', 'novice', 'superior' (and, more seriously, the realities which they express) were reduced to 'co-optation', 'newly received', 'moderator'—vague terms strongly criticised both by canonists and by theologians—and to the levelling which was surely foreign to the intention of the Council expressed in PC.

The typological definitions of the draft's Part II did not save the situation. PC § 8 had simply recognised the diversity which would have to characterise the paths towards renewal of the many different religious institutes devoted to the apostolate and left the matter there, but the descriptive canons of the 1977 draft reduced all such institutes to a few fixed categories. A number of institutes could find their place in none of them. Any religious institute not by its very nature given to works of the apostolate was to be 'monastic'. During the Council some monastic superiors wished to have monastic life identified in principle with contemplative life, but the majority of monastics, whether contemplatively oriented or not, rejected the identification as historically and really inaccurate. In the definitive text of PC, the identification was rejected. Not only were the two types of life treated separately, in PC §§ 7 and 9, but in PC § 9 a distinction was made between those monastic institutes whose members live a life including apostolic work or works of charity and those whose members live a life without them: the word 'contemplative' was avoided in speaking of both kinds. The framers of the 1977 draft, with its monastic canons intended for both contemplative institutes and monastic institutes, thus identified what the Council deliberately distinguished, and happened also to make monastics of nuns like Poor Clares and Carmelites, whose ethos and spirituality are contemplative but not monastic.

3. A LEGAL TEXT IMPLEMENTING THE COUNCIL

The typological legislation of the 1977 draft had an admirable concern: that of insuring the fidelity of different types of institute to their proper modes of existence. That concern remains in the text of 1980, but here typological difference is handled with an approach like that of LG. Canon 506, drawing heavily on the very words of LG § 46, is now among the common norms, where its function is no longer that of a basis for a particular typological classification but that of LG § 46 itself: recognition of the various formal goals of institutes of consecrated life as various legitimate ways of imitating Christ. What typological classification there is, is now that of PC, except for the omission now of monastic institutes as a distinct category. In Part III of the new Code, specific legislation for societies of common life without public vows is now provided in a Section II entirely separate from Section I with its legislation for institutes of consecrated life (i.e., those the members of which do profess public vows). Section I itself is now divided into a Title I with common norms for all institutes of consecrated life, a Title II with legislation for religious institutes properly so-called, and a Title III with twenty-one canons, almost entirely new, for secular institutes. Now that secular institutes and societies of apostolic life have their own proper legislation, the canons of Section I, Title II, are designed primarily for religious institutes. Terms like 'superior', 'novice' and 'profession' are regularly used, and the levelling feared by religious, and by members of societies of common life without vows, which are neither secular nor religious institutes, is avoided, in the spirit of PC § 1. In Section I, Title II, there is now a Chapter V on apostolate and apostolic works, and it is here that we find the typological differentiation among properly religious institutes which the new subcommission judged necessary in the Code: canon 601 defining the essentially apostolic nature of institutes given to works of the apostolate and the place of such institutes in the Church, canon 602 on lay institutes, and canon 600 on institutes disposed wholly to contemplation, which receive canonical protection from efforts to involve them in apostolic works even when necessity urges. The categories are those of PC §§ 7-11, without the monastic institutes of PC § 9, each of which may now define itself legally as wholly contemplative or partly apostolic. Elsewhere in the Code, the peculiar structures of monastic institutes are recognised.

A serious attempt has been made to apply the principle of subsidiarity, called for in the Council, in the new legislation for religious. This could be said of the 1977 draft more than of the revised text of 1980, because the new subcommission heeded the call of many religious superiors for a somewhat fuller general legislation, but in the new text much specific legislation is left to each institute, and according to canon 515 each institute is to draw up its own stable code of norms on government, discipline, admission and training of members, and objects of vows, as well as another collection of norms on matters which will more frequently need to be changed. The canons closely follow the conciliar decree *Christus Dominus* § 35, in views of exemption and in definitions of areas in which religious are subject, or are not subject, to local ordinaries. This is even more so in 1980, with 'the care of souls' added to canon 604 § 2's list of areas in which exemption does not apply, and with 'other works of the apostolate' substituted for the narrower 'external works of the apostolate' changes bringing the canon closer to the mind of *Christus Dominus* § 35, no. 4. In the revised canons regulating the periods of novitiate and of temporary profession several norms of the post-conciliar instruction *Renovationis causam* have been incorporated into the Code, and the more precise instructions on the way to proceed in processes of dismissal made available unofficially in recent years by the Sacred Congregation for Religious and Secular Institutes now appear publicly, and helpfully, in the Code.

On the whole, the new, and practically final, text is even closer to the mind of the Council than was the draft of 1977. It confuses less what should be distinct, while safeguarding those aspects of consecrated life, and of the life of societies of common life without public vows, which have real juridical consequences and which thus need a properly juridical regulation which the authors of the conciliar documents themselves did not intend to provide.

PART III

Missed Opportunities?

Hartmut Zapp

Traditions of Church Order and the Revised Code of Canon Law

THE TASK of the Pontifical Commission for the Revision of the Code of Canon Law, established on 28 March 1963 by John XXIII, was established more precisely by Paul VI on 20 November 1965. Its job was first of all to adapt the norms of the Church's code of law to a legal situation that had already altered in many respects and to the changed situation in the Church. Certainly this is one of the tasks imposed on it. Thus for example, as Benedict XV had already prescribed in vain, the changes in the law since 1918 resulting from instructions and decrees from the various Roman Congregations or from the responses of the Papal Commission for the Interpretation of the Code of Canon Law[1] are to be incorporated in the Code. Along with these are the numerous completely new laws that have been issued since the Code of Canon Law came into force, mostly in the form of letters *motu proprio*: already they fill whole volumes[2] and have to be worked into the new Church code of law. In this context consideration would also need to be paid to the numerous suggestions and criticisms which are related to the terminology or legal language and systematic structure of the Code of Canon Law and which to some extent were already to be heard just before the Code of Canon Law came into force.

Beyond this what the pope indicated the work of the canon law revision commission should above all be concerned with was to incorporate in the new Code the decisions and instructions of the Second Vatican Council and in this context to pay heed to the ten principles that should govern the revision of the Code of Canon Law approved by the Synod of Bishops on 4 October 1967.[3] Over the years that followed, drafts of the new Code were worked out, and by 15 November 1977 the entire Code existed in draft form, even though in very different stages of completion.[4] The drafts issued by the revisory commission were accompanied by hundreds of official statements by advisory bodies throughout the world and by an immense flood of publications discussing both detailed issues of the new Code as well as the general framework of whole sections. An enormous effort has so far been undertaken in connection with the revision of the Code, and its considerable benefits should in no way be belittled. Nevertheless more and more voices could be heard, including those of some bishops' conferences, rejecting the idea of a rapid promulgation of the new Code on the basis of the present state of revision and regarding a second period of consultation as necessary.

However understandable the desire may be, particularly in curial circles, for the work of revision of the future Code to be brought to a conclusion as speedily as possible, what appears equally justified on the other side is the demand for an examination whether in its present state the revised Code does justice to the situation of the Church today, a situation that in essentials is very much influenced by Vatican II. What indeed is generally recognised and established is that the new Code cannot in any way be regarded as a final and definitive formulation of Church law, even for the contemporary period, but that even today a process of continual revision and supplementation is to be foreseen, since quite simply there are too many questions that have not yet been clarified.[5] This should not in any way suggest that a code of Church law could be 'final and definitive' in the sense of never needing revision or change. On the contrary, *ius sequitur vitam*, law follows life: a good system of law must be flexible and adaptable, must necessarily grow and develop with the life of the Church, since life is dynamic, not static. But at the same time a revised code of law should at least at the moment of its promulgation do justice to contemporary needs and expectations and should not start by bringing with it an abundance of shortcomings and unsolved problems that point to the need for essential changes even before it has come into force.[6] Hence the question must be raised whether the Church is well served with such a code if there is serious ground for seeing in the process of consultation and revision that has taken place so far only the first initial steps towards a new serviceable code of Church law.[7] According to people who put forward such views not only would pastoral problems of practical theology need to be cleared up in advance, let alone purely editorial revisions undertaken on the various individual drafts, but fundamental questions about the structure of Church law and the systematic principles underlying a code of Church law would need to be investigated afresh. In this much greater consideraton would have to be paid than has hitherto been the case (if it has occurred at all) to the tradition of the history of canon law. Whether ideas of this kind are realistic and whether indeed they have even the slightest chance of being taken into consideration may, with good reason, be doubted. But that should not be any impediment to a few critical observations on the revised Code from the point of view of the history of canon law.

A first question applies to the 1917 Code. Despite the proposed arrangement of the new Code in seven books and apart from the inclusion—which still remains uncertain—of a *Lex Ecclesiae Fundamentalis* or fundamental law of the Church, this 1917 Code will continue to be valid as far as its basic conception is concerned. What understanding of canon law is it based on, what is so excellent, so timeless, so specifically ecclesiastical about it, that in general, even if with some modifications, its systematic principles are maintained? Connected with this too is the question of the place of the Code of Canon Law within the tradition of canon law.

Little research has yet been done into the history of the Latin Church's current code of law. This may be connected with the fact that both compared with the codification of civil law and also particularly within the history of canon law this Code is still very young; in addition another reason should be seen in the fact that so far hardly any access has yet been allowed to documents in the Vatican archives from the period when the Code of Canon Law was taking shape, especially the Gasparri documents.[8] Nevertheless some observations can be made about the genesis of the Code which at the same time will allow us to indicate its characteristics.

It should be undisputed that the immediate model for Gasparri and his collaborators was provided by the great European codifications of civil law that took place up to the beginning of the nineteenth century.[9] In this, French influence made itself felt most strongly; apart from the *Code civil* (*Code Napoléon*), the centenary of which was celebrated in 1904, when tribute was paid to its immense reputation by academic legal publications, Gasparri had taught for over twenty years in Paris, and alongside the suggestions of French scholars and princes of the Church this doubtless had a decisive effect on the work he contributed towards a 'modern' systematic codification of Church law.[10]

Connected with the drawing up of the Code of Canon Law *ad formam recentiorum Codicum*, on the lines of modern codes, was of course also the taking over of the concept of law tied up with these. Like them the Code of Canon Law is marked by a form of juridical conceptualisation that tends to the abstract. The Code was as a result a rationalistic codification in which legal norms were set completely free from the actual conditions of life, the chief source of law as a whole,[11] and framed in a formulation that was as abstract and absolute as possible. Behind this stood the endeavour to create a logically perfect system which was not unconnected with the idea of being able to discover or create this kind of absolutely valid and self-enclosed code out of abstract perceptions based on the 'nature' of man and of law. This kind of thinking and behaviour is above all to be traced back to absolutism. All the codes of civil law that served as models for the Code of Canon Law owed their existence to this system, are essentially marked by the spirit of absolutism, and can really be understood only on this basis; for 'to a certain extent the unlimited will of the ruler offered the technical pre-condition for codification: the idea that the absolute ruler or his delegate could fulfil every task of the law-giver, and this according to purely rationalistic considerations'.[12] One could indeed say without exaggeration that with Vatican I absolutism experienced its ecclesiastical re-animation. Papalism, with the dogma of infallibility and the extraordinary emphasis on the primatial power, linked with a continually increasing process of centralisation, now created the essential pre-conditions for an absolutist codification as far as the Church was concerned. This influence cannot only be seen very clearly in the Code itself, but is also visible in the institution, which occurred as early as 1917, of a commission for its authentic interpretation;[13] at the same time it was decreed that in the future the curial congregations should not issue any more laws, a provision that naturally could not be kept to but that clearly points to the view of Church law as *ratio scripta*, as an abstract, universal principle that hardly regards potential amendments as necessary. At best what is provided for is an authentic interpretation which is to be found only with the law-giver, i.e., the Roman Congregation. In the system of the Code of Canon Law there no longer remains, apart perhaps from marriage law, any room for the interpretation and eventual development of Church law by means of the juridical application of justice and academic canonical studies, as happened with the decretal law of the middle ages. Even if the Code's authentic interpretation has had a 'long and unhappy history',[14] it is still especially characteristic of the absolutist system with its centralising bureaucracy and administration. It is therefore not surprising to find clear parallels to this in the codifications of civil law that have been mentioned, as for example the Preussisches Allgemeines Landrecht of 1794 which provided for authentic interpretation by the Law Commission in Berlin. Further striking coincidences between the Code of Canon Law and its secular models can easily be found, ranging, among other things, from the rejection or hindrance of the formation of customary law to the style of absolutist law-giving revealed by the legal language employed.[15]

This attempt briefly to sketch the characteristics of the 1917 Code of Canon Law should not be taken as indicating a value judgment. It cannot be denied that this Code, which includes much old law among its contents, represents a great achievement and one that is widely recognised and treasured outside the Church, an achievement that rendered invaluable service to the Church and to canon law as an academic discipline. As an essentially historical entity the Church is indissolubly embedded in the conditions of each particular age; it can thus be understood that when it came to draw up its new code of law it could not shut out the views of law and tendencies that were conditioned by that age. Viewed from this aspect the Code probably represents an optimal solution; but from the other point of view attention should be drawn to the fact that after Vatican I there were, both in curial circles and in the academic world, particularly in the German school of canon law, sceptical voices raised against a codification of Church law.[16]

What is primarily at stake, however, is rather the question whether the 1917 Code must be final and definitive in the sense that even a revision of Church law today must cling to the basic conception of this Code. What must be asked is whether the tradition of canon law knows an alternative way of allowing the Church to give its law a shape for the present and the immediate future that is more convincing and better. Without a doubt the Code of Canon Law now in force meant a decisive change with regard to the canon law tradition of the middle ages. The most striking was the abandonment of the classification and treatment of the matter of canon law that had been usual in the most fruitful period of its study. Instead of this, the Code, following the appreciation of classical Roman law, of *ratio scripta*, brought about by humanism, marked a return to the classification of Gaius's or Justinian's *Institutiones*,[17] as had already been adopted by numerous codifications of civil law and by the works of canonists[18] from the sixteenth century onwards. It is noteworthy that 'despite the close connection between civil and canon law in the middle ages . . . this tripartite division—into persons, things, and actions—remained alien to classical canon law'.[19] The division of the medieval collections of decretals into five was maintained only in externals by prefacing the Code with a 'general' section and dividing actions (those arising from obligations and those arising from delicts) into two books.[20] Criticism of the Code's structure is sufficiently well known: particularly with regard to the law concerning persons it marked a 'fundamental break with the historical tradition'.[21] The revised Code may now provide for the elimination of some of the 'doctrinaire pedantries' in the present Code's Book III, *De rebus*, that have raised most objection, but essentially it clings to its predecessor's systematic structure.[22] Even canonists who agree with maintaining the fundamental structure of the 1917 Code do not refrain from justified criticism of the relevant revision so far. According to this the systematic lay-out that is envisaged, particularly with regard to the new Book II, *De Populo Dei*, 'does not do justice to the Council and in its clinging to tradition signified a regrettable step backwards'.[23]

These brief remarks about the genesis of the revised Code and the system it follows could perhaps run up against the objection that what is involved is more than merely the system underlying the revision. That is of course right. But clinging to the systematic structure that has been outlined is symptomatic of clinging to patterns of a conception of law that has probably now been superseded. Even in those few countries whose legal systems are still marked by the influence of Roman law, law and laws are no longer matters of *ratio scripta*. A code of law for the Church throughout the entire world must break away from an understanding of law that is hardly understood any longer. Apart from the often cited case of the developing countries, the historian of canon law must here draw attention to a tradition that should no longer be overlooked by a code of Church law, the common law. Its history is closely tied up with the Christian tradition of the middle ages as of more recent times, and medieval canon law did in fact play an essential part in its development.[24] Perhaps in the history of canon law there has never, since the days of the *sacri canones et decreta sanctorum patrum*, been so favourable an opportunity to attain a homogeneous canon law. The possibility exists to an extent that hardly obtained before of creating a canon law largely independent of heterogeneous legal developments, a canon law overwhelmingly orientated neither towards Justinian's *Institutiones* nor towards any other secular legal system. Referring back to the rich tradition of canon law itself could in this make more clearly explicit the fact that canon law is a system of law *sui generis*.

In its canonical formulation, a norm of ecclesiastical law must serve to make the external form of Church life recognisable and transparent. In this it must take into consideration the fact that as a historical society the Church is living in time. This means that canon law must similarly take into account social changes. Particularly in the world of today a Code of Canon Law should be marked more strongly by empirical considerations that take into account the historical and always changing situation of man and his world and do not expose themselves to the danger of overlooking the actual facts of human and Church life by clinging to abstract universal principles that rest on 'human nature'. Greater attention to the tradition of the Church would be able to make clear that for by far the major part of the history of canon law most norms can be explained historically as the Church's answers, conditioned by their age and tied to the particular situation, to the demands of its faithful.

A standard by which the revised Code must be able to be measured is to be found in the Church's most recent history, in the Second Vatican Council. With a clarity that leaves nothing to be desired the Council expounds an old principle from the history of law, that attention should be paid to the actual circumstances of life. 'The Council'—and that means the Church too—'focuses its attention on the world of men, the whole human family along with the sum of those realities in the midst of which that family lives. It gazes upon that world which is the theatre of man's history, and carries the marks of his energies, his tragedies, and his triumphs'.[25] The Council then points to the Church's special task in the service of mankind: 'To carry out such a task, the Church has always had the duty of scrutinising the signs of the times and of interpreting them in the light of the gospel. Thus, in language intelligible to each generation, she can respond to the perennial questions which men ask about this present life and the life to come, and about the relationship of the one to the other.'[26] The Church's law stands alongside the Church itself in this ministry of service for the salvation of souls. Hence the will of the Council can be interpreted as meaning that a Code of Canon Law must also respond 'in language intelligible to each generation', must take into account in its norms the changes and transformations that overtake the life of humankind and of the Church.

This principle can perhaps be quite briefly illustrated by reference to marriage law. Canon law talks of the essential qualities of marriage, deduced from the ends of this institution on the basis, so it is argued, of human nature and revelation. But over the last few decades there has been a fundamental change in our understanding of marriage, including Christian marriage. Thus the institution of marriage is no longer seen primarily as directed towards the maintenance of a people or of humankind as a whole. Against the background of medieval epidemics like the Black Death that depopulated whole regions this primary end, which the Code still clings to, is entirely understandable. But against the background of the contemporary population explosion and the threat of world over-population the *bonum prolis* must no longer be specifically protected or indeed encouraged by the institution of marriage. Marriage has similarly become meaningless for the life of the large extended family: it no longer exists. In its place marriage today is faced with new tasks and goals: its social function is completely different. Its nature is marked today by inter-personal relations, partnership and sexuality, to give only a few indications. Both the Council's pastoral constitution on the Church in the world of today and the Commission for the Reform of Marriage Law rightly sought to grasp this new vision of marriage with the idea of the *intima totius vitae communio*, an intimate partnership covering the whole of life. This raised the question whether this *amor coniugalis* was an essential component of marriage. Canonists who in the spirit of the existing Code take the view that marriage is always and everywhere essentially and necessarily the same are forced to answer 'No' to this question—and this they do. But as life shows, the institution of marriage has essentially changed, and the Church's law must take this change into account. If therefore the *bonum amoris coniugalis* (or whatever the terminology of canon law may turn out to be) is excluded, there can today be no such thing as a marriage that is valid in terms of canon law. This view should come to prevail in connection with the revised Code, and this should be seen as a welcome development. In this context the question cannot finally be excluded whether the change in the institution of marriage continues to demand the Church's clinging to the absolute indissolubility of a sacramentally contracted marriage. Naturally the decision on this matter rests solely with the Church's teaching authority. But consideration of the tradition could be helpful. The history of canon law up to the Council of Trent cannot in fact be adduced as an unequivocal support for the legal practice of the absolute indissolubility of sacramentally contracted marriages, and this applies to an even greater degree if the tradition of the Eastern Churches is also taken into consideration. Moreover, the generally prevailing view is that this indissolubility is not to be understood in the sense of a dogma (*de fide*) but is rather simply to be explained by the *bonum commune* or common good. In the historical situation that has been outlined the Church had an understandable interest in protecting marriage by means of its own particular teaching and practice. But today one would no longer be justified in talking of the institution of marriage needing protection in this way.

The suggestions sketched out here could perhaps indicate that the tradition of canon law could be of great help to the Church of today and especially to its law, due to be given a new expression, in coping better with their common task in the service of the salvation of souls. What so far cannot be established is that the work of revision of the Code of Canon Law has taken this possibility into consideration to any major extent.

Translated by Robert Nowell

Notes

1. This Commission was superseded by the Pontifical Commission for the Interpretation of the Decrees of the Second Vatican Council.

2. See the relevant collectons of T. Bouscaren, S. Meyer and X. Ochoa, and already before their time, E. Regatillo and C. Sartori.

3. See *Communicationes* 1 (1969) 86-100.

4. For a summary of the material in the context of the German-speaking world, see H. Schmitz *Reform des kirchlichen Gesetzbuches Codex Iuris Canonici 1963-1978* (Trier 1979).

5. See for example, F. G. Morrisey 'The Revision of the Code of Canon Law' *Studia Catholica* 12 (1978) 183-184.

6. See H. Schmitz *Auf der Suche nach einem neuen Kirchenrecht. Die Entwicklung von 1959-1978* (Freiburg 1979) p. 94: 'Whether the time has already come for a codification that is theologically soundly based and fully mature is a question to which an unqualified "yes" cannot be given. Too many fundamental questions still remain to be answered.'

7. On this see especially J. A. Alesandro 'The Revision of Church Law: Conflict and Reconciliation' *The Jurist* 40 (1980) 1 ff., on this point p. 13.

8. See F. Elsener 'Der Codex Iuris Canonici im Rahmen der europäischen Kodifikationsgeschichte' in A. Müller, F. Elsener and P. Huizing *Vom Kirchenrecht zur Kirchenordnung?* (Einsiedeln/Zürich/Cologne 1968) pp. 37 ff.

9. See S. Kuttner 'The Code of Canon Law in Historical Perspective' *The Jurist* 28 (1968) 139 ff.

10. Here particular mention should be made of the work by A. Pillet *Ius canonicum generale distributum in articulos* (Paris 1890); cf. F. Elsener, the article cited in note 8, pp. 38-39.

11. See S. Kuttner, the article cited in note 9, at p. 140.

12. F. Elsener, the article cited in note 8, at p. 42.

13. The Pontifical Commission for the authentic interpretation of the canons of the Code, established by the *Motu proprio 'Cum iuris canonici'*, *AAS* 9 (1917) 483-484.

14. S. Kuttner 'Ley, doctrina y jurisprudencia' in *Ius Canonicum* 11 (1971) 21, 103.

15. See F. Elsener, the article cited in note 8, at pp. 44-45.

16. See H. Lämmer *Zur Codifikation des canonischen Rechts* (Freiburg-im-Breisgau 1899) pp. 63 ff.

17. *Gai.* 1:8, *Inst.* 1:2:12: *Omne ius quo utimur uel ad personas pertinet uel ad res uel ad actiones.*

18. Above all the work by Giovanni Paolo Lancelotti *Institutiones iuris canonici*, published in 1563.

19. S. Kuttner 'Betrachtungen zur Systematik eines neuen Codex Iuris Canonici' in *Ex Aequo et Bono. Willibald M. Plöchl zum 70. Geburtstag* (Vienna 1977) 15-16.

20. See U. Stutz *Der Geist des Codex Iuris Canonici* (Stuttgart 1918) (reprinted Amsterdam 1961) pp. 38 ff.

21. S. Kuttner 'Betrachtungen', article cited in note 19, 17; for a summary of this criticism see *ibid.* pp. 16 ff.

22. See *Schema canonum libri I De normis generalibus* 4.

23. W. Aymans 'Der strukturelle Aufbau des Gottesvolkes. Anregungen zur Neugestaltung der Systematik des künftigen Codex Iuris Canonici unter besonderer Berücksichtigung des zweiten Buches' *Archiv für Katholisches Kirchenrecht* 148 (1979) 28.

24. S. Kuttner 'The Code of Canon Law', the article cited in note 9, at p. 147.

25. *Gaudium et Spes* § 2.

26. *Gaudium et Spes* § 4.

Paul Winninger

Canon Law and Catholicity

THE DRAWING up of the 1917 Code answered a practical and pedagogical need; it was useful to have a clear summary, like the Napoleonic Civil Code, of texts which had been scattered and diffuse. It was a work of scholarship, which took care to add an appendix giving the sources of the new canons. The form was new but the contents, on the whole, were not. The Decree of Gratian continued to be in force and was even reaching its zenith. The horizon was narrowly dominated by the past and Roman Catholic, in accordance with the theology and mentality of the beginning of the twentieth century.

Since then, the development of the world, and of the Church at the Second Vatican Council, has broadened perspectives. John XXIII expressed the goal to be pursued in a popular term: *aggiornamento*. In theological terms it could be translated as *catholicity* in its original sense of universality. New factors, which are elements of this catholicity which the Code must institutionalise, concern either the internal structure of the Roman Church or its new openness to other kinds of Christianity and the world.

1. REQUIREMENTS OF CATHOLICITY WITHIN THE ROMAN CHURCH

Among the marks of the Church given by the creed, the one which is most lacking is definitely catholicity. Catholicity was expressed at the Council by three rediscoveries which could develop it:

(a) The dogmatic constitution *Lumen gentium* no longer defines the Church as a hierarchical pyramid but as the people of God born through baptism. This stresses the value of the *common priesthood of the faithful* which the ministerial priesthood must not obliterate.

(b) There was also the rediscovery of the *local church* as the place where the universal church is experienced. This local church exists at two levels. First the diocese, with it precise territorial limits. But these are often artificial and the result of historical accidents. There is no common measure, for example, between the numerous tiny dioceses in Italy and the vast German dioceses. That is why the important level is usually the national one, or a cultural and linguistic unit embracing several countries. These are the ancient metropolitan divisions. Hence the setting up of national episcopal conferences between the diocesan bishop and the pope to govern these local churches.

(c) In theology as in law, the major restoration of the Council was the *collegiality of bishops*. This is exercised at two levels: at the base, to govern the national churches and at the top to join in the primacy of the pope.

This is the most promising development for the catholicity of the Church of tomorrow and also the most difficult to put into practice, because of the excessive power assumed by the papacy over more than a millenium. How are we to redefine relations between pope and Council, pope and synod? The gracious and condescending use of an absolute power supported by law is not sufficient. And how can we reconcile the arbitrary nature of the reservation of certain questions to the Holy See with the affirmation of collegiality, which is exercised in practice by episcopal conferences, synod and Council? Collegiality should operate on essential questions. Otherwise it is empty of substance and incapable of ensuring the life of the Church. It should operate, for example, on the question of ministries, the nomination of bishops, the liturgy.

The new canon law must therefore first organise catholicity within the Roman Church. Catholicity in this sense is opposed to all forms of narrowness or power grabbing. It is defined in practice by harmony between the three major institutions of the Council: the common priesthood of the baptised, the autonomy of the local church and the collegiality of bishops. Logically it should result in the concerted setting up of three legislative levels:

diocesan synodal statutes which are a traditional institution. After the Council, most of them fell into disuse. Very few dioceses are thinking of redrafting them, because this seems premature in a rapidly developing situation. The growing poverty of priests necessitates improvisations and attempts outside the mainstream of current law, but perhaps these are the beginnings of a future law;

a regional or national law at the level of episcopal conferences would be a novelty comparable to the laws of the Eastern Churches united with Rome. The infrequent national synods since the Council have defined the elements of such a law. But here too the instability of the situation has resulted in an opportunist empiricism;

a law for the whole Roman Church—this is doubly risky. It might either restore a burdensome Roman centralism in the void left by the lack at the two previous levels, or it might leave the details to diocesan and national law and remain at the level of generalities, a sort of framework of law-enunciating principles.

A major tension of our time in all areas, is the difficult search for a balance between global uniformity encouraged by the speed of communications and technical requirements, and the instinctive need for regional or national identity, which is fiercely opposed to anonymous submersion. The Church, which began with Pentecost, has the secret of conviviality in diversity. The 1917 Code was a fairly poor illustration of this. Will the new legislation be any better? The suppression of distance by air travel, telephone and radio can support two opposite arguments. The technologically rational conclusion leads to centralism in politics, uniformity in technology and conformism in culture: as a whole, to tyranny and the death of the mystery of the personal. On the other hand, truly human rationality argues from the speed of communications to the possibility, which used to be much more difficult, of respecting the greatest possible autonomy and variety, without fear of deviations since these can be corrected and stopped in time. Authority can become more supple without any danger of collapsing.

Respect for catholicity in space by law, has as its complement *catholicity in time*. Another tension which is more serious in law than anywhere else, is how to reconcile fixity and development. Laws are nearly always established as if they were meant to be permanent. But life, particularly in this century, is dynamism and evolution. Hence the doubts and major criticisms of the project of drawing up a new Code such a short time after the Council. Hence the suspicion that this enterprise would be a hasty restoration of a status quo. Nothing would be more surely doomed to failure. This is one of the very rare laws of history. Life goes forwards and it is never possible to go backwards. The question therefore is how, in what terms, by what preliminary dispositions, could the law itself decree its temporary character and periodical revision.

The compilers' attitude to the past and the future should be governed by this same catholicity in time. The insistence on the permanence, until the middle of this century, of the Decree of Gratian, which is a compilation of texts from another world, another millenium—the dark ages—and which has ruled over the Christian people like a super-gospel, is both a radical vice of the falsely religious spirit, denounced by Jesus in the Pharisees who were fixated on a superannuated law, and a superstition, ignorance posing as knowledge. It is time to get rid of this heavy erudition and look to life and the gospel, draw up a Code, in which the parish is no longer a benefice, a Code which tries to build the Church of tomorrow. Perhaps it is too much to ask jurists to be prophets, but we can suggest that they should invite some theologians, sociologists and pastors to their editorial committees. There is a need to integrate the past, which is now better known, thanks to the research of recent decades, and the future, the signs of which are already apparent in people's lives today. These are the catholic pre-requisites to a new Code within the Roman Church.

2. ECUMENICAL AND WORLD CATHOLICITY

But true catholicity is wider. It extends to all Christians and embraces the churches separated from Rome. It is convenient to call this dimension the ecumenical. Furthermore, Christians have always understood the Good News of Jesus Christ as universal, addressed to all people: this is full catholicity. Can the new Code in some way express these two aspects of catholicity? This is a difficult, perhaps unexpected question. Is it beside the point? It is easy enough to reply that the Code only concerns Roman Catholics. To those outside, it bears witness and conveys an image: will it show a closed spirit or an attempt to meet and ways to make this meeting happen?

(a) Especially for the separated churches, the new Code will be a major test of Rome's ecumenical progress. People measure and perceive closeness or distance far more by laws, which they experience and which are applied in the parish (e.g., mixed marriages, intercommunion), than in the theoretical formulation of articles of faith. At the base, among the faithful, disciplinary disagreement is more strongly felt than doctrinal divergence. The open-minded texts of Vatican II (The Decree *Unitatis redintegratio*) need to find not only a verbal response, but application in legislation on important problems: the exercise of the primacy of Peter, ministries, marriage, sacraments, intercommunion. We need a composition which successfully avoids hardening into a system and proclaims the unity of the Church, which all Christians desire. Especially in Church organisation and the exercise of power, the Orthodox Church and the Reformation Churches have long practised the decentralisation recommended by Vatican II and have autonomy or autocephaly at three levels: diocese, nation and supreme head. Ecumenism has no future unless the Roman Church commits itself boldly to this course.

(b) It would also be an excellent thing, in the spirit of the Declaration *Nostra aetate* (on non-Christian religions) and the Constitution *Gaudium et Spes* (the Church in the modern world), to introduce a *truly universal dimension* into this Code. In particular, reference to the Decree *Ad Gentes* (on the Church's missionary activity) must affirm the Church's respect for the cultures and customs of non-Christian peoples, as opposed to missionary behaviour in the past, which was sometimes narrow and iconoclast. This behaviour was thoroughly 'uncatholic' and the modern traveller through the world can see its grievous results.

True catholicity is universality without totalitarianism. It is in the order of mystery, that is to say, of grace. If it is pursued by purely human means, it results in the founding, not of a Church in the spirit of Christ at Pentecost, but of a sect, even though it may be a world-wide sect.

This, we must admit, is the great temptation of the Roman Church. It remains to be seen whether the Code will succeed in embodying this Catholic ideal and in changing a practice, which remains to this day, destitute of any serious ecumenical, let alone universal, hope.[1]

Translated by Dinah Livingstone

Note

1. See Charles Wackenheim *Le Pari catholique* (Paris 1980).

Richard Potz

Is the Language of the Draft Codex Intelligible and Contemporary?

I

THE CRISIS of religious language today is—whatever one may feel about it—a generally accepted fact to which this journal has more than once in the past turned its attention.[1] Nor is there any need to spell out the fact that this crisis particularly affects the two linguistic levels of canon law, *the language of the Church's law* and *the language of the discipline of canon law*. The main difficulties have affected the language of canon law itself, that is the language in which the canonical rules (which, of course, in the main take the form of laws) are formulated. The burden of the universal criticism of juridicalism has been, in effect, that the wholesale creation of legal norms out of statements which derive their meaning from the level of religious language leads to a distortion of the meaning of those statements by confusing linguistic levels. This difficulty creates a consequent problem for the language of the discipline of canon law, that is the language in which statements are made about the theory, methodology and content of law in the Church, namely that of finding a third level on which to bridge the gulf between religious language and legal language.[2] The discipline of canon law was given the task of implementing the wishes of Vatican II on the linguistic level of jurisprudence, for example by producing statements establishing basic rights, general rights of participation by the faithful, improved legal safeguards, etc. The great congresses of canonists in the last ten years have shown what has been done in this area, but also what still remains to be done. It is in this situation that we now face a comprehensive codification.

No attempt to come to terms with the existing draft Codex can avoid the obvious linguistic problem resulting from this phase of unrest and movement and from the arguments at the academic level, many of which are only now beginning. What criteria for *contemporaneity* and *intelligibility* can be found and developed?

One premiss must be that the normative character of legal language gives laws, and in particular a general code, an important temporal quality: codes are produced with the intention that they will remain fixed for long periods. The history of canon law itself gives us eloquent testimony to this. As is well known, Pope Benedict XV declared at the presentation of the CIC (*Codex Iuris Canonici*) on 28 June 1917; 'As the inheritor of his (Pius X's) authority, we intend to promote the faithful observance of the law and will close our ears to any demand for any declaration of invalidity'.

But how can a comprehensive code be contemporary in a period marked by constant movement resulting from real or supposed crises? If we start from the traditional view of the function of codes referred to by Benedict XV, the question is very simply answered: the Code checks the movement, overcomes the crises and so creates a stable and manageable situation. This view corresponds to a widespread expectation. It was expressed at a very early stage of the work, as can be seen from a remark of Cardinal Felici's at the 50th anniversary celebrations for the CIC on 27 May 1967. The cardinal expressed the hope that '. . . the new Code will be . . . the best guardian of the spirit of the Council and contribute—as we hope—to the restoration of internal peace in the Church'.[3] In other words, codification coincides with the end of the phase of post-conciliar experimentation.[4]

On the other hand, the contemporary character of the new Code could also be measured by the extent to which it guarantees dynamic development of the law. This, however, presents an incomparably greater challenge to linguistic formulation. In general legal terminology this would mean a choice of general instead of casuistical, and also unspecific as opposed to specific formulation.[5] Casuistical formulation is more comprehensive, more detailed, but also has more gaps; the scope for adapting the law to particular cases is small. General formulations are shorter, leave fewer gaps and give the body responsible for specific applications of the law greater discretion. In other words, the degree of generality of a rule determines the size of its area of application, the number of real situations it covers. There is no necessary connection between these terms and the terms 'specific' and 'unspecific'. Experience of casuistical legal language has led to a widespread acceptance of the advantages of general formulations, but the insistence on clarity as a general principle is still generally maintained. It should be emphasised at the start that neither clarity nor precision, nor indeed intelligibility, necessarily suffers from the generality of the terms. 'Diocese' is certainly more intelligible than 'particular Church', but 'particular Church' as a general term is more intelligible than the terms used for the 'sub-Churches' similar to dioceses ('free abbey', 'free prelature', etc.). Nevertheless the intelligiblity of all these terms is—if we ignore the fact that, ecclesiologically, the diocese is the ideal form of the particular Church—about equal.

Specificity means that one can be certain in predicting the application of the norm: unspecific formulations usually have a wide area of indeterminacy alongside the core of their field of application in which criteria for the application of the rule can be found only in the individual case.

For our purposes it is important to remember that the Church's law code has certain features which require an extensive use of unspecific regulations. If the Church's laws are to be based on the spirit of Vatican II, if the new codification of canon law is to be 'the best guardian of the spirit of the Council', the 'provisional openness' of the conciliar statements should not be crushed by detailed rules. The frequently invoked spirit of the Council can be reflected only by an open legal language which deliberately takes the risk of unspecific formulation.

Legislation and legislative development which does justice to this outlook must be based on the premiss that the provisions of the law are guidelines. The underlying point here is that the linguistic structure of many conciliar statements is optative; they are intended to initiate and sustain developments, to open up new areas of active responsibility for the faithful in the Church and in the world. If these intentions were transformed into over-specific imperatives, in such areas the codification would stop or limit such developments. In contrast to the general theory of law-making, which has strong reservations about evolutionary laws that merely provide direction, under the circumstances mentioned here unspecific 'evolutionary' legal language is to be welcomed in many areas in the new codification of canon law. At the same time, however, it would seem important that, in accordance with the optative character of the Council's statements, the *aims* should be formulated with some precision, while the various alternative *implementations* may be left open and unspecific. Even if this gives the rule the character of an ideal, the reference to the aim seems to me to provide a sufficient degree of force for specific applications.

An example. Canon 709 runs:

'§ 1. Totius Colegii Episcoporum et Sedis Apostolicae imprimis est promovere et dirigere participationem catholicorum motui oecumenico, cuius finis est plenam unitatem doctrinae inter omnes Christi discipulos parare et sic unitatem Ecclesiae redintegrare.

§ 2. Episcopis item est, et ad normam iuris Episcoporum Conferentiis, eandem promovere, atque pro variis adiunctorum necessitatibus vel opportunitatibus, normas practicas statuere, attentis praescriptis a suprema Ecclesiae auctoritate statutis.'

(§ 1. It is the duty of the whole episcopal college, and in particular of the Apostolic See, to promote and direct the participation of Catholics in the ecumenical movement, the aim of which is to bring about full doctrinal unity among all the disciples of Christ and so to restore the unity of the Church.

§ 2. It is also the responsibility of bishops, and of episcopal conferences within the limits of their powers, to promote this participation and to lay down rules of practice as different needs and occasions arise, subject to the regulations issued by the supreme authority of the Church.')

This is a law with a quite specific statement of aim, but unspecific formulations of possible implementations within the limits of standard rules of competence.[6] In addition to the delegation of responsibility to the particular legislator, this canon introduces an important interpretative rule for the development of canon law, the obligation to adopt an *interpretatio oecumenica*, to interpret all rules of canon law in an ecumenical spirit.

I shall now briefly mention two more examples of relatively general and unspecific formulations from marriage law. Canons 1049 and 1052 depart from the CIC in formulating incapacity and malicious deception as new grounds for nullity. Canon 1049 mentions persons 'qui ob gravem anomaliam psychicam obligationes matrimonii essentiales assumere nequeunt', ('who, because of a severe psychological anomaly, are unable to assume the essential obligations of marriage') and c. 1052 includes under the constituent elements a character 'quae nata est ad consortium vitae coniugalis graviter perturbandum', ('so constituted as serious and disrupt the partnership of married life'). In view of the generality and unspecific character of these two canons we may expect that development in the Church's law on marriage will be centred mainly on them. In the case of incapacity this phenomenon is of course already familiar, and there have been detailed arguments over it between tribunals and academics. In the case of the formulation of 'malicious deception' it remains to be seen how the tribunals will interpret in specific cases the casuistical and restrictive definition: 'deceptus dolo, ad obtinendum consensum patratus . . .'.

It will thus be seen that the draft Codex contains a large number of formulations whose generality and unspecific character offer some hope that the new Code will be fairly long-lasting. However, this welcome tendency in the draft should not blind us to the fact that large sections are dominated by canons taken word for word from the CIC or that newly written canons in the main follow the traditional lines of the technique of codification.

What at first seems a remarkable reduction in the number of canons from 2424 to 1728 is mainly the result of the radical excision of penal and procedural provisions (a reduction of 231 and 266 canons respectively). This means that what would be an important indication of a more general, less casuistical formulation, namely the reduction of canons in the relevant sections of *De normis generalibus, De Populo Dei, De Ecclesiae munere docendi, De Ecclesiae munere sanctificandi* and *De bonis Ecclesiae temporalibus*, when allowance is made for new institutions, does not exceed 20 per cent.

To the extent that the draft is no more than an adaptation of the CIC, it may be expected that after a short period of stabilisation, longed for by many, the movement of the development of law will continue, bypassing canons defined in excessive casuistical detail or that the gulf between the ecclesial community and its law will widen to such an extent that the Code will become an abstract and bloodless structure that will live only in academic discussions.

II

The literature on the CIC constantly stresses that the number of legal definitions is extraordinarily large. This used to be justified in the main by the claim that technical canonical language suffered from severe terminological uncertainty. This gave the CIC to a marked degree the character of a manual, which was very convenient for the rules about its use in teaching.

If the technical language of canon law was uncertain, this is now no longer so and with its disappearance has disappeared the need to incorporate definitions. Interestingly, however, legal definitions have not been abandoned, but it has been seen as one task of the new codification to incorporate fundamental conciliar statements as legal definitions, so that the draft sometimes has the air of a manual of post-conciliar canon law. Notable examples from the general provisions are the definition of law (c. 7), of the different forms of administrative acts (cc. 29 ff; 25; 48; 49; 59), of privilege (c. 76), of a legal person (c. 110), and many others. There are encyclopaedic definitions of truly classical proportions for *Christifideles* (c. 201), particular Church (combined with a list of examples, c. 355!), life according to the evangelical counsels (c. 503) and marriage (c. 1008).

Judged by the history of the movement for codification, the draft Codex represents a pinnacle in the consistent incorporation of definitions. It is clear that this is an attempt to make the work as contemporary as possible, and in particular to meet the criterion of renewing canon law in the spirit of Vatican II, but it nevertheless gives the Codex an overall impression of finality and conservatism.

III

It is impossible to talk about the intelligibility of the draft without a brief final discussion of its legal Latin. In general there is no reason to change the comments made in the literature on the legal language of the 1917 CIC: 'A Latin without ornament, plain and sober, but fluent and precise, hardly ever leaves the specialist, even on a cursory reading, in doubt about the true meaning of the particular provisions.'[6] In some cases, primarily in the case of the incorporation of lengthy formal definitions (see above), a more emotional tone will be felt, but it should not be forgotten that in many cases this fulfils an important function: this technique is generally welcomed for formulations of basic law in civil codes too! And conversely it has been possible in many cases to eliminate well-known drafting errors and unnecessary imprecisions, as a comparison with Mörsdorf's fundamental work on the legal language of the *Codex Iuris Canonici* makes clear.[7]

As the quotation in the last paragraph indicates, the Latin of the draft will be intelligible to the specialist, but is that enough? In the general legal discussion about the intelligibility of legal language opinions are divided. Should laws as far as possible be intelligible to those to whom they are addressed? Or should they at least correspond to the language of one stratum of society or be formulated in a language current in a particular stratum? Or is it really enough if the legally trained specialist understands the language of the laws?

The use of Latin as the language of law gives all these considerations an added dimension. For students of the legal language of the 1917 CIC there seemed to be no objection to the use of Latin: 'In secular law codes an effort is rightly made to some extent to use ordinary language; the Swiss Civil Code is an example of this. Only for the general canons of the Church, which are drawn up in a dead language and addressed primarily to the leaders of the Church, need this not be a requirement' (Mörsdorf).[8] The first and most obvious question here is whether we would want to maintain the premiss that the general canons of the Church are addressed primarily to the leaders of the Church, or whether we should aim at intelligibility among a large number of those to whom the laws are addressed. If our premiss is that—as has already been mentioned several times—the task of the new codification is to renew canon law in the spirit of Vatican II, there can be no doubt about the answer to this question. A way must be found to bring canon law close to those to whom it is addressed, and that is all the faithful and not just the leaders of the Church.

For the codification to be drawn up in Latin as the 'authentic language' is the only defensible approach to carrying out this intention in legal procedure. This, however, will make it no less necessary to make the text of the laws accessible to those governed by it in suitable translations. There is no difficulty in solving the problems this creates. Lawyers have experience of them already, and, indeed, are constantly facing them through the necessity of translating international treaties, which are drawn up in one or more authentic languages. And apart from the fact that officially approved translations of the conciliar documents already exist, translation ought to be made easier by the relatively standard terminology which the discipline of canon law has already created in the various languages.[9]

To summarise, an examination of the legal language of the new Codex shows the following. Despite many happy formulations the theoretical objections to a new codification of canon law in general and at present in particular have not been removed. The specific character of the provisions and the large number of dogmatic definitions indicate the intention to use the Code to bring the phase of post-conciliar renewal to an end. This is to make the law's main function not only to provide a stay for the travelling people of God but to make them—certainly only temporarily—stay put.

Translated by Francis McDonagh

Notes

1. See the articles in *Concilium* 113 (3/1978), and especially Schillebeeckx 'The Crisis in the Language of Faith as a Hermeneutical Problem' *Concilium* 85 (1973) 31-45.

2. On the theoretical and methodological basis of this section, see R. Potz *Die Geltung kirchenrechtlicher Normen Prolegomena zu einer kritisch-hermeneutischen Theorie des Kirchenrechts* (Vienna 1978).

3. '. . . il nuovo Codice di leggisarà la migliore tutela dello spirito del Concilio e contribuirà—così speriamo—alla restaurazione della pace interna della Chiesa.' *Communicationes* 1 (1969) 58.

4. As when Pope John Paul told Major Women Religious Superiors from all over the world that the period of post-conciliar religious experiment was now over and that, for the orders, 'the time has come to assess the experiments undertaken objectively and humbly in order to recognise the positive elements and any errors and to work out a stable rule of life approved by the Church. . . '. See *Österreichisches Archiv für Kirchenrecht* 31 (1980) 183.

5. For the references to the general theory of law-making in the rest of this article see esp. P. Noll *Gesetzgebungslehre* (Reinbek, Hamburg 1973), esp. pp. 244 ff, and the contributions in *Studien zu einer Theorie der Gesetzgebung* ed. J. Rödig (Berlin, Heidelberg, New York 1976).

6. On the problems of legal language created by the provisional openness of the conciliar statements, see Potz, in work cited in note 2, at p. 167 ff.

7. U. Stutz *Der Geist des Codex Iuris Canonici* (Stuttgart 1918) p. 47; see also R. Köstler *Wörterbuch zum Codex Iuris Canonici* (Vienna 1927) p. 9; K. Mörsdorf *Die Gesetzessprache des Codex Iuris Canonici* (Paderborn 1937), esp. pp. 25 ff.

8. Mörsdorf, the work cited in note 7.

9. Mörsdorf, *ibid.* p. 18.

Communication

Charter of the Rights of Catholics in the Church

THE ARCC (Association for the Rights of Catholics in the Church, P.O. Box 3932 Philadelphia, PA 19146, (215) 925-6946) was founded in March 1980 with the purpose to bring about substantial structural change in the Catholic Church. It seeks to institutionalise a collegial understanding of Church in which decision-making is shared and accountability is realised among Catholics of every kind and condition. It affirms that there are fundamental rights which are rooted in the humanity and baptism of all Catholics. To this end the association will develop and implement a Charter of the Rights of Catholics in the Church.

The ARCC has begun a process to draft such a charter (Magna Carta Catholica) on a world-wide basis. In each country suggestions from individuals and groups will be received by a committee, read, and synthesised. The results will then be forwarded to the international drafting committee. The resulting document will be submitted for approval by the collaborating committees, and the process of obtaining the Charter's discussion and adoption throughout the Church will begin.

To build a framework for this charter, the major studies in this domain have been analysed. From this analysis a random listing of what might be included in a Charter was developed. The following provisional list is proposed to help interested individuals and groups submit lists of rights they think might be incorporated into an international Charter of Catholic Rights.

1. Human rights, which people have because of their dignity as human persons, rights they do not lose on becoming Catholics: personal rights, rights relating to the family, rights in society; as the right to: Life; Physical and mental integrity; Personal development; Travel and residence; Equality and non-discrimination; Reputation and good name; Personal dignity; Privacy; Act according to one's own conscience; Free choice of state in life; Marriage and family life;

Professional activity; Self-determination in temporal affairs; Participate in social and economic decisions; Artistic and cultural freedom; Work for justice and peace; Promote human rights.

2. Ecclesial rights, which Catholics have because they are members of the Church. These are based on their dignity as baptised persons: personal rights as Catholics; rights related to the Word of God; rights related to sanctification or the means of becoming holy; rights related to the mission of the Church; as the right to:

Religious liberty; One's own rite in the Church; Association; Assembly; Seek the truth; Hear the Word of God; Profess the Faith; Spread the news of salvation; Information; Formation; Education (at all levels); Inquiry into the sacred sciences (theology); Share results of this inquiry; Teach the Faith; Publication and freedom of the Press; Public opinion; Dissent;

Communion; Unity; Prayer; Spiritual goods Christ gave the Church; Pastoral care; One's own spirituality; Active participation in the Liturgy; Sacraments; Holy life; One's own apostolate; Use one's own charisms and skills; Exercise charity.

3. Ecclesiastical rights, which are tied to the legal structure of the Church: rights as individuals in the Church; rights to certain activities or benefits within the institutional life of the Church: as the right to:

Express needs to Church authorities; Express opinions in and about the Church; Petition; Initiative; Support the work of the Church; Collaborate in the work of the Church; Mutual accountability; Legitimate and adequate development of hierarchical activities; Appeal to the hierarchy; Be consulted; Vote; Decent working conditions for Church workers; Just wage for Church employees.

4. Right to the protection of rights in the Church; as the right to:

Protection of one's rights; Redress to vindicate one's rights; Fair administrative procedures; Due process in any effort to restrict one's rights.

Contributors

AELRED CODY was born in Oklahoma City (USA) in 1932, and is now a priest and a monk of St Meinrad Archabbey. Doctor of Sacred Theology (Ottawa) and of Holy Scripture (Rome), Diplômé de l'École Biblique et Archéologique Française (Jerusalem), Associate of the Royal College of Music and of the Royal College of Organists (London), he has been professor of holy scripture in St Meinrad Seminary (Indiana, USA) 1967-68, then in Sant'Anselmo and the Pontifical Biblical Institute (Rome) 1968-78. He is a member of the Oriental Orthodox-Roman Catholic Consultation in the United States 1981-   . His publications include: *Heavenly Sanctuary and Liturgy in the Epistle to the Hebrews* (1960); *A History of Old Testament Priesthood* (1969) and various articles in *Biblica, The Catholic Biblical Quarterly, Revue Biblique, Theological Studies, Vetus Testamentum, Proche-Orient Chrétien, L'Orient Syrien, The Journal of Egyptian Archaeology, Theologische Realenzyklopädie, A New Catholic Commentary on Holy Scripture, Dizionario degli Istituti di Perfezione.*

THOMAS GREEN gained his licentiate and doctorate in canon law at the Gregorian University, Rome, before becoming successively assistant professor and associate professor of canon law at the Catholic University of America, Washington DC. He is chairman of the Canon Law Society of America Task Force on the Revision of the Code and a member of the Canon Law Society of America Editorial Board for Commentary on New Code. He has written various articles on the proposed revisions of the Code of Canon Law.

RUUD HUYSMANS was born in Eindhoven in the Netherlands in 1935. In 1959, after his seminary training, he was ordained priest in the diocese of Rotterdam. From 1960 to 1966, he studied canon law at the Lateran University in Rome. His thesis, most of which was published in the *Ephemerides Iuris Canonici* of 1967 and 1969, was on the history in canon law of the impediments to mixed marriage. In 1967, he was appointed professor of canon law in the Catholic School of Theology in Amsterdam. Since that time, he has published articles in various scientific journals, and one book, *Tussen concilie en synode. Overhet ontwikkelen van de kerkstructuur door de nederlandse bisdommen vanaf 1966* (Hilversum 1981).

JOSEPH KHOURY was born in Lebanon in 1936, and ordained in 1964. He studied at the Gregorian, Urbanian and Lateran Universities in Rome. He now teaches Oriental canon law, sacramental theology, history of Islamic philosophy and Arabic and Syriac in Rome. Since 1969 he has been a member of the Sacred Congregation for the Eastern Churches. He is author of *Jurisprudence de la S. R. Rota dans les causes des Eglises Orientales*, 2 vols. (Rome 1972), and of a manuscript Introduction to the history of Islamic philosophy.

JOSEPH KOMONCHAK was born in Nyack (New York) in 1939 and ordained in 1963. He studied philosophy at St Joseph's Seminary, Yonkers, NY, and theology at the Gregorian University in Rome from which he received the licentiate in sacred theology in 1964. After serving in a parish for three years, he taught systematic theology at St Joseph's Seminary for ten years. In 1976 he received his doctorate in philosophy at Union Theological Seminary, New York, with a dissertation on the ecclesiology of the young Newman. Since 1977, he has been an associate professor in the Department of Religion and Religious Education at the Catholic University of America, Washington, DC. His publications include various articles on the *magisterium*, the theology of liberation, the ordination of women and ministries in the Church in various theological journals.

PETER LENGSFELD was born in Breslauc Wroclaw) in 1930, and after having gained a licentiate and doctorate in theology at the Gregorian University in Rome he did pastoral work in Berlin between 1958-61. In 1964 he became qualified to teach dogmatics and ecumenical theology in Münster and since 1967 he has been professor of ecumenical theology and director of the Catholic Ecumenical Institute of the University of Münster.. His published work includes *Überlieferung. Tradition und Schrift in der evangelischen und katholischen Theologie der Gegenwart* (Paderborn 1960; also Fr. and Span.); *Adam und Christus* (Essen 1965; also Fr.); *Das Problem der Mischehe* (Freiburg 1970); *Ökumenische Theologie. Ein Arbeitsbuch* (ed., Stuttgart 1980). He is co-editor of the journal *Una Sanca*, and a member of the European Societas Oecumenica.

RICHARD POTZ was born in Vienna in 1943 and studied law and Byzantine and Eastern European history at the University of Vienna. He was awarded the doctorate of laws in 1965 and in 1972 was recognised as a university lecturer in canon law in the Faculty of Jurisprudence and Politics; since 1977-78 he has been acting professor of canon law. Dr Potz has made a special study of Eastern canon law, and in 1978 he was appointed a consultor to the Vatican Commission for the examination of Eastern canon law. In 1979 he was made a full member of the Viennese Catholic Academy. His principal public works are *Patriarch und Synode in Konstantinopel—Das Verfassungs-recht des Ökumenischen Patriarchats* (Vienna 1971) and *Die Geltung kirchenrechtlicher Normen—Prolegomena zu einer kritisch-hermeneutischen Theorie des Kirchenrechts* (Vienna 1978).

JAMES PROVOST was born in 1939 in Washington, DC. Ordained a priest at Louvain (Belgium) for the diocese of Helena, Montana (USA), he gained a doctorate in canon law at the Lateran University in Rome in 1967. He served as chancellor and officialis of the diocese of Helena from 1967 to 1979, and currently serves as assistant professor of canon law at The Catholic University of America. President of the Canon Law Society of America in 1977-1978, he is now executive co-ordinator of the Society and directs its permanent seminar on research in canon law and theology. He is managing editor of *The Jurist* and edits the *Proceedings* of the Canon Law Society of America. He has published various articles on canon law and on pastoral issues.

HERWI RIKHOF was born in 1948 in Holland. Having studied theology in Utrecht and Oxford, he graduated in 1981 under Professor Schillebeeckx with the thesis: *The Concept of Church; a Methodological Inquiry into the Use of Metaphors in Ecclesiology*. Since 1979 he has been scientific assistant at the Theological Institute of the University of Nijmegen.

REMIGIUSZ SOBAŃSKI was born in 1930 in Tarnowskie Góry, Poland, and ordained priest in 1954. He has doctorates in theology and law and is currently professor of the constitutional law of the Church in the Canon Law Faculty of the Academy for Catholic Theology in Warsaw, of which he is currently pro-rector. His publications include *Chrzest jako podstawa jedności Kościoła* (Baptism as the Basis of the Unity of the Church, Warsaw 1971), *Zarys teologii prawa kościelnego* (Outline of the Theology of Canon Law, Warsaw 1973), *Kościół—prawo—zbawienie* (Church—Law—Salvation, Katowice 1979) and numerous articles in both Polish and western journals.

PAUL WINNINGER was born in 1920 in Michelbach (Haut-Rhin, France). He is a priest of the diocese of Strasbourg, and has been parish priest of Gunstett since 1979. He has been professor of philosophy since 1946, and was formerly head of department in the Faculty of Catholic Theology at the University of Strasbourg. His latest work is *Ordonner des prêtres* (Paris 1977).

HARTMUT ZAPP was born at Säckingen in 1939. His further studies after he had gained his degree included a period at the Institute of Medieval Canon Law, which at that time was still attached to Yale. He is a *Privatdozent* for canon law and the history of canon law at the Institute of Canon Law of the University of Freiburg-im-Breisgau. His publications include articles in periodicals and encyclopedias as well as *Die Geisteskrankheit in der Ehekonsenslehre Thomas Sanchez* (Cologne 1971).

The following extract from an interview with Cardinal Pellegrino of Turin is published here by the express wish of the editorial board of *Concilium*, decided on the occasion of their recent annual general meeting held in Cambridge, England:

Question: Don't you see what straits our theologians are in?

Answer: In my opinion we have to acknowledge the contribution theologians make and the role they play and we must work with them. There's so much to be done. I fear that we're in a blind-alley. And some people are prepared to admit this, in private.

Question: So it's a question of not having the courage to speak out?

Answer: Yes, that's it, and it isn't the first time.

Question: How would you explain this fear?

Answer: Oh, well, perhaps it's a false understanding of humility, or a certain conception of obedience, or perhaps, who knows? What is certain is that what is called in the Bible 'outspokenness' (*parrhesia*) is not much in evidence in today's Church. This outspokenness can, of course, be misused so that the authorities become worried. But we shan't get anywhere by standing still. The Church must go forward, and it must go in the direction of the Council.

Question: But you must be aware that theologians are being watched and that cardinals and bishops are afraid?

Answer: Yes, that's sad, very sad. Poor Church! How far we are from the 'Yes, yes', 'No, no' of the Gospel. In my next book I write about the 'Warning Letters' that bishops get through the post. Bishops are ordered to stop certain theologians from speaking. But why shouldn't the individual bishop decide this for himself? This smacks to me of real interference on Rome's part. I can understand that a bishop should think it's inopportune for such and such a theologian to speak in his diocese; what I can't understand is that he should be ordered to take this measure from above. Freedom isn't respected enough in the Church. I do understand that there should be anxiety about turmoil in the Church or damage to it, but I think that such anxiety has negative consequences and is exaggerated. There's no freedom of speech and writing. If only the bishops took up their responsibility, the Roman curia would tread more softly. Let's talk with each other before we invoke the 'power of holy obedience'! If only each bishop would take time to reflect rather than fall immediately into line whenever he is inclined to take the voice of Rome for the voice of God. I've dug in my heels myself before now. . . .

From an interview with Cardinal Michele Pellegrino of Turin with Francesco Strazzari, published in *Il Regno* on 15th April 1981.

CONCILIUM

Claude Geffré. 0 8164 2542 6 144pp.
The Future of Christian Marriage. Ed. William Bassett and Peter Huizing. 0 8164 2575 2.
Polarization in the Church. Ed. Hans Küng and Walter Kasper. 0 8164 2572 8 156pp.
Spiritual Revivals. Ed. Christian Duquoc and Casiano Floristán. 0 8164 2573 6 156pp.
Power and the Word of God. Ed. Franz Bockle and Jacques Marie Pohier. 0 8164 2574 4 156pp.
The Church as Institution. Ed. Gregory Baum and Andrew Greeley. 0 8164 2575 2 168pp.
Politics and Liturgy. Ed. Herman Schmidt and David Power. 0 8164 2576 0 156pp.
Jesus Christ and Human Freedom. Ed. Edward Schillebeeckx and Bas van Iersel. 0 8164 2577 9 168pp.
The Experience of Dying. Ed. Norbert Greinacher and Alois Müller. 0 8164 2578 7 156pp.
Theology of Joy. Ed. Johannes Baptist Metz and Jean-Pierre Jossua. 0 8164 2579 5 164pp.
The Mystical and Political Dimension of the Christian Faith. Ed. Claude Geffré and Gustavo Guttierez. 0 8164 2580 9 168pp.
The Future of the Religious Life. Ed. Peter Huizing and William Bassett. 0 8164 2094 7 96pp.
Christians and Jews. Ed. Hans Küng and Walter Kasper. 0 8164 2095 5 96pp.
Experience of the Spirit. Ed. Peter Huizing and William Bassett. 0 8164 2096 3 144pp.
Sexuality in Contemporary Catholicism. Ed. Franz Bockle and Jacques Marie Pohier. 0 8164 2097 1 126pp.
Ethnicity. Ed. Andrew Greeley and Gregory Baum. 0 8164 2145 5 120pp.
Liturgy and Cultural Religious Traditions. Ed. Herman Schmidt and David Power. 0 8164 2146 2 120pp.
A Personal God? Ed. Edward Schillebeeckx and Bas van Iersel. 0 8164 2149 8 142pp.
The Poor and the Church. Ed. Norbert Greinacher and Alois Müller. 0 8164 2147 1 128pp.
Christianity and Socialism. Ed. Johannes Baptist Metz and Jean-Pierre Jossua. 0 8164 2148 X 144pp.
The Churches of Africa: Future Prospects. Ed. Claude Geffré and Bertrand Luneau. 0 8164 2150 1 128pp.
Judgement in the Church. Ed. William Bassett and Peter Huizing. 0 8164 2166 8 128pp.
Why Did God Make Me? Ed. Hans Küng and Jürgen Moltmann. 0 8164 2167 6 112pp.

109. Charisms in the Church. Ed. Christian Duquoc and Casiano Floristán. 0 8164 2168 4 128pp.
110. Moral Formation and Christianity. Ed. Franz Bockle and Jacques Marie Pohier. 0 8164 2169 2 120pp.
111. Communication in the Church. Ed. Gregory Baum and Andrew Greeley. 0 8164 2170 6 126pp.
112. Liturgy and Human Passage. Ed. David Power and Luis Maldonado. 0 8164 2608 2 136pp.
113. Revelation and Experience. Ed. Edward Schillebeeckx and Bas van Iersel. 0 8164 2609 0 134pp.
114. Evangelization in the World Today. Ed. Norbert Greinacher and Alois Müller. 0 8164 2610 4 136pp.
115. Doing Theology in New Places. Ed. Jean-Pierre Jossua and Johannes Baptist Metz. 0 8164 2611 2 120pp.
116. Buddhism and Christianity. Ed. Claude Geffré and Mariasusai Dhavamony. 0 8164 2612 0 136pp.
117. The Finances of the Church. Ed. William Bassett and Peter Huizing. 0 8164 2197 8 160pp.
118. An Ecumenical Confession of Faith? Ed. Hans Küng and Jürgen Moltmann. 0 8164 2198 6 136pp.
119. Discernment of the Spirit and of Spirits. Ed. Casiano Floristán and Christian Duquoc. 0 8164 2199 4 136pp.
120. The Death Penalty and Torture. Ed. Franz Bockle and Jacques Marie Pohier. 0 8164 2200 1 136pp.
121. The Family in Crisis or in Transition. Ed. Andrew Greely. 0 567 30001 3 128pp.
122. Structures of Initiation in Crisis. Ed. Luis Maldonado and David Power. 0 567 30002 1 128pp.
123. Heaven. Ed. Bas van Iersel and Edward Schillebeeckx. 0 567 30003 X 120pp.
124. The Church and the Rights of Man. Ed. Alois Müller and Norbert Greinacher. 0 567 30004 8 140pp.
125. Christianity and the Bourgeoisie. Ed. Johannes Baptist Metz. 0 567 30005 6 144pp.
126. China as a Challenge to the Church. Ed. Claude Geffré and Joseph Spae. 0 567 30006 4 136pp.
127. The Roman Curia and the Communion of Churches. Ed. Peter Huizing and Knut Walf. 0 567 30007 2 144pp.
128. Conflicts about the Holy Spirit. Ed. Hans Küng and Jürgen Moltmann. 0 567 30008 0 144pp.
129. Models of Holiness. Ed. Christian Duquoc and Casiano Floristán. 0 567 30009 9 128pp.
130. The Dignity of the Despised of the Earth. Ed. Jacques Marie

Pohier and Dietmar Mieth. 0 567 30010 2 144pp.
131. Work and Religion. Ed. Gregory Baum. 0 567 30011 0 148pp.
132. Symbol and Art in Worship. Ed. Luis Maldonado and David Power. 0 567 30012 9 136pp.
133. Right of the Community to a Priest. Ed. Edward Schillebeeckx and Johannes Baptist Metz. 0 567 30013 7 148pp.
134. Women in a Men's Church. Ed. Virgil Elizondo and Norbert Greinacher. 0 567 30014 5 144pp.
135. True and False Universality of Christianity. Ed. Claude Geffré and Jean-Pierre Jossua. 0 567 30015 3 138pp.
136. What is Religion? An Inquiry for Christian Theology. Ed. Mircea Eliade and David Tracy. 0 567 30016 1 98pp.
137. Electing our Own Bishops. Ed. Peter Huizing and Knut Walf. 0 567 30017 X 112pp.
138. Conflicting Ways of Interpreting the Bible. Ed. Hans Küng and Jürgen Moltmann. 0 567 30018 8 112pp.
139. Christian Obedience. Ed. Casiano Floristán and Christian Duquoc. 0 567 30019 6 96pp.
140. Christian Ethics and Economics: the North-South Conflict. Ed. Dietmar Mieth and Jacques Marie Pohier. 0 567 30020 X 128pp.

1981
141. Neo-Conservatism: Social and Religious Phenomenon. Ed. Gregory Baum and John Coleman. 0 567 30021 8.
142. The Times of Celebration. Ed. David Power and Mary Collins. 0 567 30022 6.
143. God and Father. Ed. Edward Schillebeeckx and Johannes Baptist Metz. 0 567 30023 4.
144. Tensions Between the Churches of the First World and the Third World. Ed. Virgil Elizondo and Norbert Greinacher. 0 567 30024 2.
145. Nietzsche and Christianity. Ed. Claude Geffré and Jean-Pierre Jossua. 0 567 30025 0.
146. Where Does the Church Stand? Ed. Giuseppe Alberigo. 0 567 30026 9.
147. The Revised Code of Canon Law: a Missed Opportunity? Ed. Peter Huizing and Knut Walf. 0 567 30027 7.
148. Who Has the Say in the Church? Ed. Hans Küng and Jürgen Moltmann. 0 567 30028 5.
149. Francis of Assisi: an Example? Ed. Casiano Floristán and Christian Duquoc. 0 567 30029 3.
150. One Faith, One Church, Many Moralities? Ed. Jacques Pohier and Dietmar Mieth. 0 567 30030 7.

All back issues are still in print and available for sale. Orders should be sent to the publishers,

T. & T. CLARK LIMITED
36 George Street, Edinburgh EH2 2LQ, Scotland